Mentoring Doctoral Students in Higher Education:
An International Perspective

EMERALD: INTERNATIONAL HIGHER EDUCATION

SERIES EDITORS:
Fredrick. M. Nafukho, Texas A&M University
Beverly Irby, Texas A&M University

Published Titles

Training School Principals as Talent Developers:
  An International Perspective (2022)
  Sonya D. Hayes, Nahed Abdelrahman,
  Beverly Irby, & Fredrick. M. Nafukho

Global Issues and Talent Development:
  Perspectives from Countries Around the World (2018)
  Khali Dirani, Fredrick. M. Nafukho, & Beverly Irby

Cultural Impact on Conflict Management in Higher Education (2018)
  Nancy T. Watson, Lei Xie, & Matthew J. Etchells

Conflict Management and Dialogue in Higher Education:
  A Global Perspective (2nd Edition) (2017)
  Nancy T. Watson, Karan L. Watson, & Christine A. Stanley

Talent Development and the Global Economy:
  Perspectives from Special Interest Groups (2017)
  Fredrick. M. Nafukho, Khali Dirani, & Beverly Irby

Governance and Transformations of Universities in Africa:
  A Global Perspective (2014)
  Fredrick. M. Nafukho, Helen M. A. Muyia, & Beverly Irby

Mentoring Doctoral Students in Higher Education: An International Perspective

BY

MICHAEL F. BURNETT

Louisiana State University

United Kingdom – North America – Japan – India – Malaysia – China

Emerald Publishing Limited
Emerald Publishing, Floor 5, Northspring, 21-23 Wellington Street, Leeds LS1 4DL

First edition 2025

Editorial matter and selection © 2025 Philip E. Bernhardt, Ofelia Castro Schepers, and Megan Brennan

Individual chapters © 2025 The authors.

Published under exclusive licence by Emerald Publishing Limited.
Reprints and permissions service

Contact: www.copyright.com

No part of this book may be reproduced, stored in a retrieval system, transmitted in any form or by any means electronic, mechanical, photocopying, recording or otherwise without either the prior written permission of the publisher or a licence permitting restricted copying issued in the UK by The Copyright Licensing Agency and in the USA by The Copyright Clearance Center. Any opinions expressed in the chapters are those of the authors. Whilst Emerald makes every effort to ensure the quality and accuracy of its content, Emerald makes no representation implied or otherwise, as to the chapters' suitability and application and disclaims any warranties, express or implied, to their use.

British Library Cataloguing in Publication Data

A catalogue record for this book is available from the British Library

ISBN: 979-8-88730-847-0 (PB)
ISBN: 979-8-88730-848-7 (HB)
ISBN: 979-8-88730-849-4 (EPDF)

CONTENTS

Dedication vii
Acknowledgments ix
Preface xiii
Introduction xvii

1. Cutting Your Teeth: A Painful Process 1
2. Like Hell You Will!! 5
3. The Value of Determination and Persistence 9
4. The Right Topic 13
5. Motivated! 15
6. Beware of Manipulator 19
7. Honesty 25
8. Experiences 29
9. Is Desire Enough? 33
10. Plagiarism—Oh My!! 37
11. Hard Heads 43
12. Handicaps 47
13. The Green-Eyed Monster 51
14. Sometimes You Can Trust the Cover 57
15. Ability Is Not Enough 61
16. See You When You Get Back—Personal Priorities 81
17. References 85

DEDICATION

This book is dedicated to the two people who first taught me the meaning of honor, integrity, honesty, and true caring.

The first I would mention is my paternal grandfather (I called him Pa.). During the early years of my life, my dad (who had only a high school diploma) worked as much (including overtime) as he possibly could to provide for his family. Consequently, he was not there as much as he would have liked to be or as I would have liked him to be. However, I probably did not miss his presence so much because my Pa was always there. Pa taught me about the importance of having a strong work ethic, he taught me about the importance of being honest and always behaving in an honorable manner. He taught me about the true meaning of the saying "A man is only as good as his word." He taught me all these things not by the words he said but by the example he set.

A little later, my family's financial situation became a bit more stable, and my dad was able to spend more time with me. This is when I really got to know my dad. My dad cared about his family more than words can express, but my dad cared about everyone. Because of this he freely volunteered his time to work with boys' church groups (mostly the RA's – Royal Ambassadors), consequently, much of my time with my dad was with 10 to 20 other young boys. I would probably have been more jealous had it not been for my growing relationship with Pa.

I guess the true nature of my dad's caring did not become really clear to me until I was about 17 years old. My dad had accepted a pastorate at a small church in a community located in my hometown of Spartanburg, South Carolina. This was in 1978 in the Southern United States. Racism was rampant, and a group of Black Christian men were going to White churches and attempting to go in and join the Sunday morning worship service. Whether or not they were allowed to enter they never caused a disruption. If they were allowed to join the service, they simply sat on the back pew quietly until the service ended. They then thanked the minister and left. If they were not welcomed, they just left quietly. These Christian men were met with everything from locked doors to hostile threats. One day our church was in a business meeting after the Sunday morning service, and one of the deacons brought up the issue and proposed that we needed to devise a strategy for the best way to keep these Black men out if they tried to come into our church. The words that my dad said to the church membership are inextricably burned into my brain. I remember them as if he said them yesterday. He said,

> Anyone who wants to come into our church and worship with us is welcome, and the day that this is not true is the day that I am no longer your paster!

What a testimony! We lost members over his statement, and we were a stronger and better church without them. My dad always took the position that bigotry and hatred are always wrong but nowhere more so than in the church.

These and many other examples of honor, integrity and caring are why this book is dedicated to my dad and my Pa.

ACKNOWLEDGMENTS

There are many people that I really need to acknowledge for having helped me to reach the point that I was able to write this book.

First, of course are my Pa and Dad. I will not say much here since the book is dedicated to them.

Secondly, I must acknowledge the individuals in my life that not only taught me about what a true mentor is but showed me as well.

Dr. John Rodgers was both my undergraduate and master's degree advisor and mentor. Dr. Rodgers was one of the most honorable men that God ever placed on this Earth, and it is impossible to adequately express what his advice, his mentorship and his example meant to me. Truly, 10 years into my career in higher education, every time I was faced with a BIG decision, I would call and talk with Dr. Rodgers. Of course, he never told me what to do, but just talking with him helped me see things more clearly.

When I entered my doctoral program, I figured that people like Dr. Rodgers would be noticeably absent. However, what I found was Dr. J. David McCracken, Dr. L.H. Newcomb, and Dr. J. Robert Warmbrod.

Dr. McCracken was assigned as my major professor, and I could not have asked for a better person to fill that role. He was an honest, decent, caring man. In other words, he was honorable. He directed me through my doctoral program and helped me to avoid the "land mines" that can cause a person to experience long delays or even failure. I truly appreciate him for this. I learned MANY things about being a good doctoral advisor that I still use today.

Dr. L. H. Newcomb was one of the members of my general exam committee. At Ohio State at that time, a doctoral student had two committees – one for the general exam and then another committee for the dissertation. The second committee was called a writing committee, and it did not have to be the same people except for the major professor. When I went to LH to ask him to be a member of my writing committee, he told me that he did NOT believe in what I was studying, however, he said, "But I believe in YOU, so if you want me to be one the committee I will for YOU!" I called him about a year before I found a publisher for this book and asked him if he would be willing to read the book and give me feedback. He said that he had been retired for several years and that not a week went by that he did not get a request similar to mine. He said that thus far he had never accepted one. However, he said, "But if you want me to review your book I will do so because I believe in you!" How could I ever live my life without caring about people when I have these types of examples that have shown me the way through their lives.

I MUST acknowledge the contributions of Dr. J. Robert Warmbrod. Dr. Warmbrod was the other member of both my general exam committee and my writing committee. Dr. Warmbrod passed away about a year ago, and our profession lost the most influential individual that has ever worked in our field. I dare say that you could not go into any Agricultural Education program in the United States without finding the influence of Dr. Warmbrod. Dr. Warmbrod taught a sequence of research courses when I entered the program at OSU, but he moved into administration and soon ceased to teach the courses. In fact, I had the entire sequence of four courses, the last time he taught them all. The semester I was enrolled in the first research course, there were 250 students in the course. Based on the program enrollment and the students that were early in their program, the most AGED students that could have been enrolled in the course was about 25-30. Students came from all over campus to take his courses. The word was on the OSU campus that if you could not understand research when Dr. Warmbrod taught it, you might just as well quit and go home. Dr. Warmbrod was the BEST teacher I have ever had the pleasure to know. It was his influence that made me understand what I wanted to be. It was at the break midway through the second session of the first in his sequence of courses, and I was standing in the hall on the second floor of the Agricultural Administration Building at OSU when I had an epiphany. I knew at that moment that I wanted to do what Dr. Warmbrod did. I wanted to teach research and I wanted to do it as well as he did. Well, my friends and even faculty told me, don't expect to be able to teach research right away. In most AGED programs in the nation, it is generally reserved for the "Elder Statesman" in the program. At our first faculty meeting just before the beginning of the Fall 1980 semester at LSU, we were discussing course assignments, and Dr. Charles W. (Billy) said, "I do not know what else you will be teaching this Fall, but you WILL be teaching that damned research course, because I have been teaching it and I hate it!" In good old Brer Rabbit fashion, I said, "Please don't throw me in that briar patch," and I 43 years later, I am still teaching it and four other course I modeled after Dr. Warmbrod's sequence of courses at OSU. Now, I tell my students every semester that everyone who does not get to learn research from Dr. Warmbrod is being cheated. I have accepted that I will never be half the teacher that he was, but I DO keep trying! I would be happy if I could just reach the halfway point of the teacher that he was. I wish he were here to read this because I do not know if I ever told him just how much he meant to me.

Another acknowledgement that is essential is the students with whom I have worked these 43 years. I have directed 172 doctoral dissertations (one completed as recently as last Friday) and 30 master's theses. Without exception, each of these students has been truly outstanding. We had a professor in Education at one time that taught statistics to all our doctoral students, and she told me that our students were her favorite ones to teach. When I asked her why, her response pleased me but honestly did not surprise me that much. She said it was their work ethic. She said that our students were not necessarily brighter than others, but she never worried about them being successful because she knew they would work at it until they got it.

I would truly love to recognize some of my very best students by name, but I am not sure where I would stop, and you really do not want to read a list of 200 plus names. I do not know why my students ascribe so much of their success to me, but I tell them that one common flaw among all my students is that they give me WAY too much credit for their success, and they ARE successful. I have had a doctoral graduate who was 29 years old when she finished her doctorate and a student who was 62 when she finished. Let me just suffice e it to say that I do not know why such wonderful students have come my way, but I am truly thankful for each and every one of them.

I would also be remiss if I did not acknowledge my wife (Ann) and my three daughters (Kara, Lauren, and Hope) for their patience and understanding with having to share my caring and concern for them the way I did with my dad. I wish there had been a Pa here to fill in the holes. I do love each of them more than I can express with mere words, and I fear that there have been times when they perceived reasons to doubt that. Please know that I love each of you beyond words, and I could not have been successful without your love and support.

Thank you.

PREFACE

Before I begin telling you about the lessons that I have learned while working as a doctoral advisor, I should probably tell you just a little about myself and a few of my experiences that may qualify me to say some things about doctoral advising and mentorship.

I was born in 1951, which of course tells you that I have at least had the opportunity to have had a lot of experience. Early in my academic career, I heard a highly respected high school principal from Washington State make the comment that when examining the experience of the teachers you are supervising, you must distinguish a teacher who has 25 years of experience from one who has one year of experience 25 times over. I have not been able to recall or locate his name or I would give him appropriate credit for this comment; but, in any case, I do not claim it as original with me. This comment caused me to carefully examine my career and the things that I had learned from my experiences thus far. One very important aspect of this is to learn from the mistakes that you make, but I think it also means to learn from the successes you have. I promised myself that from that point I would try to learn something from all my doctoral advising experiences, and I think I can truthfully say that I have accomplished this purpose. But I digress, so let me get back to telling you a little about my background.

I grew up in Spartanburg, South Carolina in the 1950s and 60s. This is actually about two-thirds correct. My home in Spartanburg was rather typical of that time. It was multi-generational since my maternal Grandmother came to live with us before I was born, and she brought with her my mother's nephew. My cousin lived with us until he was grown, and my grandmother lived with us until a severe stroke forced her into a nursing home. My Dad had a high school diploma and was a veteran of World War II. Actually, he did not see fighting, but he was stationed in Japan in the occupation forces after the atomic bombs were dropped on Hiroshima and Nagasaki which led to Japan's surrender. In the first six or seven years of my life, my Dad worked in the rail yards for the Southern Railway Company, and he loved his work. The railroad companies went through some very difficult times in the mid to late 1950s, and my Dad often found that his work was in another town at least and often in another state. Additionally, on occasions he went through periods when there was no work in Spartanburg and because of this he was temporarily laid off. My Mother was adamant that she would not move from Spartanburg, and so after a brief time in Kentucky, followed by six months without work my Dad sought other employment. He found a job with the United States Postal Service and spent the rest of his working life as a postal clerk. He hated the job from the day he started it to the day he retired from it some 30 years later. I remember as a small child overhearing a conversation between my parents about my dad returning to the Railroad when they called him back. My Dad clearly wanted to go, but my Mother said (very nearly if not a quote) "Do what you want, but I can remember Doris [my younger sister] crying because we did not have money to give her a mayonnaise sandwich." My Dad never looked back. Not only this, but he accepted as many hours of overtime as possible to provide us with the things we needed and wanted. Consequently, my Dad was not around a lot in my younger years.

The other third of my young life was spent with my paternal grandparents. They lived on a small farm in a tiny town called Moore, South Carolina just outside of Spartanburg, and they (especially my grandfather) ingrained in me many of the values that I still live by today. My Grandfather was of the period when a man's word was his bond, and if he shook hands on something, he considered that to be as binding as any legal contract in the world. I will share one story that exemplifies the kind of person who taught me much of my early values.

This happened when I was about 16 years old, and I was getting ready to go to my grandparents' farm for the weekend. My Grandfather called me and asked me to stop at the feed store and pick up a bag of horse feed. I did not realize until I was in the store that I did not have enough money to pay for the feed, and the man in the store that knew me was not working that afternoon. I learned later that the man who helped me was the owner of the store. I told the man my situation and told him that I had my checkbook, but I did not have the cash to pay for the feed. I asked if he would take my check. He said, "that depends—Who are you?" I told him my name and that my Grandfather (Weldon Burnett), was the one who asked me to stop and get the feed. He asked, "So, Weldon Burnett is your grandfather?" to which I replied, "Yes sir." The next words that he said have stayed with me from that day. He said, "Son, if Weldon Burnett is your Grandfather, you can write me a check for the whole store if you want to because I know he would make it good." This is who I learned my values from as a young boy.

Clearly my Grandfather was my first real mentor, and when I talk about things throughout this book that involve value judgements, you will now have some understanding of the foundation of those value judgements.

I graduated from high school in 1969 while the Vietnam War was very hot, and I applied to and attended Clemson University. In that time, finishing your degree in four years was not an option if you wanted to delay your entry into the U.S. Army. I joined the Air Force through the ROTC program, but never really spent much time on active duty. This was because we pulled out of Vietnam at about the time, I was scheduled to begin my active-duty stint in the Air Force.

I finished my baccalaureate degree in 1973, and I graduated with my master's degree in 1974 at which time I started teaching high school in Greenville County at Southside High School. After teaching high school for three years, I went back to graduate school at The Ohio State University (in 1977) from which I graduated with my Ph.D. in August 1980. My experiences at OSU were truly exceptional and laid a great foundation for the things I did professionally the next 40 plus years.

I joined the faculty at Louisiana State University (LSU) in August of 1980 and was assigned my first doctoral advisee soon after my arrival. Over the next 43 years since then, I have served as the committee chair for 127 doctoral students who have graduated with a Ph.D. and 27 master's students who have completed the thesis option in the program. Therefore, I have been officially listed as the major professor/committee chair for 154 students who have completed and successfully presented to their graduate committees a doctoral dissertation or master's thesis. Additionally, I served in the unofficial capacity of directing the dissertation/thesis for 45 doctoral students and 21 master's students for whom I was not identified as the committee chair or co-chair. Among these were six students in the School of Social Work and three in the College of Education. I have been very careful to include only those students for whom I filled this role who (I have very strong confidence) would identify my role in their study if asked to do so. Therefore, I have directed more than 220 graduate studies in the last 43 years. Of these dissertations directed seven were in programs in the College of Education, six were in the School of Social Work and one was on a committee for which I was serving as the Graduate School Dean's Representation. Twice, I was even asked to assist with dissertations that were being conducted at Ohio State by currently employed instructors at LSU. One of these requests came from a former committee member at OSU and the other came from a colleague at LSU. I also directed two dissertations for students on whose committee I was not even included as a member. One of these was in our program and the other was in the School of Social Work here at LSU.

In addition to my role in directing dissertations and theses, I have served as a member of 197 doctoral advisory committees. Included among these committees were:

- Eleven on which I served as the Graduate School Dean's Representative,
- Four on which I served as a Minor professor,
- Seven committees in the School of Social Work,
- Six committees in the College of Education,
- Two in the School of Human Ecology,
- One in the Department of Communication Studies, and
- Two on which I was not officially a member of the committee but directed the dissertation research (one in our School and one in the School of Social Work).
- I have also served on 21 master's thesis option committees.

Generally speaking, students completing M.S. degrees in the non-thesis option in the Program are not very demanding of time. This is not to say that they are unimportant, and there are, of course, exceptions to the amount of time involved in assisting a student through the non-thesis option. Just for the sake of the record, I have served as M. S. Graduate Advisory Committee Chair for 92 students (seven of whom were in the College of Education). Additionally, I have served as a member of 144 master's committees in my 43 years at LSU. Seven of these students were in the College of Education, two were in the Department of Experimental Statistics, one was in the School of Human Ecology, and I served as the minor professor on one of these 144 committees.

All told, I have been a part of more than 450 student dissertation/theses committees with almost half of these in a capacity of directing the study. This equates to more than 10 committees per year and about five per year in the capacity of directing the study. If the nonthesis master's committees are counted, I have been part of almost 650 graduate advisory committees in the last 43 years.

The organization of this book is focused on selected lessons that I have learned during the past 40 plus years that I feel would be particularly beneficial to a person embarking on a role as a doctoral advisor. At no point in this book is a specific person, especially a student, identified by name in the book. It is possible that some of the individuals discussed in the book may recognize themselves if they choose to read the book; however, no one is named in the book except for some of the faculty members who directed my studies, and those who are identified are always done with the greatest of respect and appreciation for the things they have done to help me in my life and career.

INTRODUCTION

Many people who decide to pursue a doctorate have a very specific career path in mind when they enter a doctoral program. Some of these know they want to work in the world of academia. After more than forty years in this career, I can tell you without hesitation or reservation I am very happy that this is the path I chose. I am certainly not suggesting that everything is perfect in higher education, because it is not. You first must find a position, hopefully one in a place where you want to work. When I entered my doctoral program at The Ohio State University, my sole purpose was to return to Clemson University where I completed my first two degrees and spend my career there emulating my academic mentor (Dr. John H. Rodgers). If I were just going to choose a climate in which to work, I would not have chosen South Louisiana. Some people say that we have three seasons in South Louisiana—Warm, Hot, and Blast Furnace. Add to that the fact that hurricane season runs through the Blast Furnace season. It took a long time for me to get accustomed to the weather here. I will say that going to work on a bright sunny morning in January with the temperature 45 degrees and going up to 65 during the day makes up a lot for the Blast Furnace weather of July through September. You will probably find, like I did, that the climate is not nearly as important as the work and the people.

Mentoring Doctoral Students in Higher Education:
An International Perspective, pages xvii–xix.
Copyright © 2025 *Michael F. Burnett*
Published under exclusive licence by Emerald Publishing Limited
ISBN: 979-8-88730-847-0 (PB); 979-8-88730-848-7 (HB); 979-8-88730-849-4 (EPDF)

If you land your position in academia, you must then work diligently toward achieving tenure. One of my former administrators was wont to say that the best job in higher education is a tenured full professor, and I believe he was right. If you want to be successful in this first position, you should do as much as you can to achieve the skills and abilities needed to be successful while you are enrolled in your doctoral program. For example, my area was agricultural teacher education. That means that if/when I got a position as a beginning assistant professor in one of the Agricultural Education programs in the nation there were certain things that I should expect to do as part of my job. These things included:

1. Teach undergraduate courses,
2. Advise undergraduate students,
3. Supervise student teachers,
4. Teach graduate courses,
5. Advise graduate students,
6. Design and conduct in-service programs for teachers in the field,
7. Serve on departmental, college, and university committees,
8. Etc.

Many of these things I sought specific experiences to gain the needed preparation before I left OSU. For example, I had teaching experience (at the high school level), so I was not so concerned about teaching undergraduate students. However, I had never supervised a student teacher in the field, so I requested and was given the opportunity to get direct preparation in this area. I also sought and was provided with experience teaching graduate courses, not as the instructor of record but teaching specific lessons for my major professor's courses. I even had the opportunity to serve as a student member of the graduate council during my last year at OSU. This was a great experience.

One of the things your doctoral institution cannot really provide you is the opportunity to advise graduate students, especially doctoral students. I helped several of my fellow students at OSU design, analyze and report their findings, but I was their friend, not their supervisor. It is a very different role. I have always heard throughout my education that the knowledge and understanding needed to do something and the knowledge and understanding needed to teach something are vastly different. I can assure you that nowhere is this more undeniably true than in graduate advising, especially doctoral advising. Most people think that since they have successfully completed a dissertation, directing a student through the process should be a proverbial "Piece of Cake." I promise you it is not!! However, I can say without any hesitation that doctoral advising has been for more than forty years the best part of my career. This career activity like many of the best things in life, had a rocky start, and some of the roads it has taken me down have been very bumpy.

Driving on these roads for more than forty years has taught me some very valuable lessons. Many of these lessons have been learned at a considerable expense of time, stress, and occasionally personal anguish. My purpose in writing this book has been two-fold:

1. First, I hope that people who read this book may be able to learn from my lessons and consequently become effective doctoral advisors much more quickly than I did. It is worth the effort, but only if you do it well.
2. Secondly, I personally needed to write the book. I have become the doctoral advisor that I am today through the synergistic effects of interacting with all my former students as well as my friends and colleagues both here at LSU and at numerous other universities around the country and even the world. I have been promising myself for 10 years that I was "someday" going to write a book about graduate advising. Putting this in written form has helped me to synthesize all the things I have learned through this aspect of my career and gain a deeper understanding of myself. Therefore, even if this book is not subsequently published, it has been a great experience for me personally. During the time that the university was closed because of COVID-19, I spent many hours on my back patio, writing, sometimes until dark.

While some of the lessons were learned from experiences with one specific student, most of them are a compilation of experiences with multiple students.

This book is organized in a "generally" chronological order, but when I felt the need, I have drawn from experiences with students throughout my career. The first lesson in the book is drawn directly from the experiences with my first doctoral student and for a very good reason. I think it will become evident when you read the first chapter. One thing that I sincerely hope is evident throughout the book is my unwavering belief in the value of effective mentoring. In my opinion, this is something that has been seriously damaged in our age of mass production and immediate gratification. You cannot become an effective mentor in a few sessions. It takes a lot of time and effort.

One of my dearest friends in the world is a colleague with whom I worked for many years. He has been retired now for several years, but he has continued to be one of my most cherished friends and mentors. A few years ago, my friend's wife (who is also one of my dear friends) hand-stitched a beautiful picture of a cardinal sitting on a flowering tree limb and gave it to me for a Christmas present. The picture is beautiful, and I treasure it. It has a place of prominence on the wall in my office. However, the note that she gave me with the picture is even more treasured. She starts my saying, "I wanted to thank you for being my husband's mentor." As he is a true elder statesman in our program, I always considered him my mentor. The following words in her note helped to affirm the worthiness of the doctoral advising aspect of my efforts over these last 40 plus years: She said that we (I and her husband), ." . . help students to go out in the world as blessed human beings and spread knowledge to the next generation."

CHAPTER 1

CUTTING YOUR TEETH: A PAINFUL PROCESS

It was during my first year at LSU when I was assigned my first doctoral student. He was an international student, which was not problematic for me since he spoke impeccable English, and almost half of the doctoral students at Ohio State, during the time I was enrolled in my doctoral program, had been from a wide variety of other countries. This young man was very bright, but he was also very introverted to the point that he rarely spoke up in class, and for the most part accepted authority as absolute. Within a few months after he was assigned to me, another new doctoral student was assigned to me as an advisee also, but the focus of this section is on the first student. I worked with him as closely as I was encouraged to do so, and I sought a lot of advice from the other members of the faculty in my department, especially Billy. Billy had been at LSU for quite some time, was a Louisiana native, had gone north to Pennsylvania State University for his doctoral program many years earlier, and was designated as the Assistant Director of the School in which my department was housed. This student went through the coursework portion of his doctoral program pretty much without incident, and then with a lot of help from Billy, I managed to direct him successfully through his general examination. At LSU, the exam that takes place at the end of

Mentoring Doctoral Students in Higher Education:
An International Perspective, pages 1–4.
Copyright © 2025 *Michael F. Burnett*
Published under exclusive licence by Emerald Publishing Limited
ISBN: 979-8-88730-847-0 (PB); 979-8-88730-848-7 (HB); 979-8-88730-849-4 (EPDF)

a student's coursework is called the general examination; and, in our program, it consists of both a written and oral component. The written component involved at that time (and still does) a set of questions submitted from each of the members of the student's doctoral advisory committee. The student had to respond to these questions in a manner designated by each member of the committee, but for the most part they were done "in-house" without the use of any resources. Additionally, the student was expected to complete the entire set of questions in one day. I felt that it was imperative that I follow the procedures used in the Department, after all, I was the new kid on the block, and I had only been there about two years when my first student was doing his exam. That means that I was not yet tenured and was to be reviewed for the continuation of my appointment during my third year. I did not really think that it was a good time for me to fight the accepted procedures. Additionally, when we were discussing a problem with our student teaching coursework (specifically, the fact that students were enrolled in one twelve credit hour course which meant that there was very little ability to make fine differentiation among grades assigned to the students because, at that time, LSU did not have plus/minus grading), and I mentioned that the way Ohio State addressed this problem was . . . It was at this point that one of the faculty members in our department stopped me and informed me that people here at LSU did not consider Columbus, Ohio to be Mecca, and we do not care how they do it there. That was the last time for many years that I said this is how they do it at Ohio State. I did, however, suggest and get passed setting up a group of three credit hour courses (like OSU) instead of one 12 credit hour course so that faculty members could interject more differentiation in the students' grades. I guess it really IS all in the presentation.

Doctoral advisory committees at that time consisted of six faculty members. So, my student wrote his examination on one day starting from early in the morning to late that evening, and when I learned that he had not even had a lunch break, I promised myself that I would not allow another one of my students to have this experience, and I did not. From then on, I had all the committee members to submit their written exams to me, and I had the student write one committee member's questions per day for a series of days. I thought this was a much more reasonable way for the exam to take place (That is how they did it at Ohio State, but I did not say that.), and I think my students performed at a higher level without the extreme fatigue associated with writing for such a long, sustained period. Anyway, my student got through the general examination successfully, and then my learning experience started. Up to that point, I was just more or less doing what Billy told me to do; however, when it came time to start the dissertation, I learned how ill prepared I really was for this component of my faculty role. Since the student had never done a dissertation before (of course not), and I had never directed a dissertation before, it was the proverbial "Blind leading the Blind," and the student's career was on the line. I had completed a dissertation, but I fell far short in terms of having the knowledge and understanding needed to direct a student through this process. I sought as much help as I could, but by this point, Billy had left the Department to accept an administrative position, and his hands were full. We were searching for a faculty member to replace him, and the faculty member who was just a couple of years ahead of me knew less about working with doctoral students than I did (if that is possible). The absolute best advice I could give to a faculty member advising his first doctoral student is to identify the best, most highly sought-after doctoral advisor in your department, and ask that person to co-chair your first doctoral advisee's committee with you. You will be amazed at how much YOU will learn.

Well, my student got his proposal approved, collected his data (after a couple of hiccups), and was writing his dissertation. However, things were not going well; and I am compelled to admit that it was not the student who was to blame for this; it was me. I just did not know how to effectively teach him to construct a dissertation. I had done mine only a few years before, but that was not helping much. My student was planning to graduate in December 1983, and we finally came to the point when I just had to say to him that his dissertation was just not ready to present to his committee. The student was furious, and I can well understand why. He had done what I told him to do, and he knew that; but I just did not know how to tell him to get it right. In 1964, the United States Supreme Court Justice Potter Stewart in talking about obscenity made the comment that "I know it when I see it" (Stewart as cited in Gewirtz, 1995–1996). Well, I could have said about my student's dissertation—that I know a good dissertation when I see it, and at least at that point, his dissertation was not it. Unfortunately, it was my job to help him get his dissertation to that point, and I had failed at my job.

The student was very frustrated, especially because his family was coming from his home country to see him graduate in December, and now I had told him that he would not be graduating until at least a semester later. This quiet, shy young man called me a lot of very uncomplimentary things using some language that was the first time I had been called those things, at least to my face. The thing that I am most ashamed of in this incident is what I did next. In his barrage, he told me that I did not know what I was doing and that he would have to hear from his committee that the dissertation was not ready, and I said, okay then go ahead and take it to your committee. From that time, any student who asks me to be their major professor must accept one primary rule: The dissertation does not go to the committee until I say it goes to the committee. If they cannot accept this rule, I tell them to find someone else to chair their committee, and that there will be no hard feelings. There have been a few situations when a student was pushing, and I reminded them of this rule. I offered to step down; but, to this point, I have not had one to take me up on the offer.

My first student did eventually graduate but not until he had presented his dissertation to his committee three times! I wish that I could see him one more time just to tell him how sorry I am for the things I put him through. I have never let another student goad me into an exam for which they were not ready. Oh, I have had some that have had rough exams, but not because I knowingly let them walk into a lion's den completely unprepared. One of the things I tell my students today is that we do not go to the final exam (dissertation defense) until I am ready to vote to pass them regardless of what the rest of the committee does. It is not the student against the world, it is me and the student against the world. Well, it sounds better when I tell it to the student.

Cutting new teeth can be a very painful process. Try to be sure that the one experiencing the pain is the one cutting the teeth. Do not use your first student(s) as a chew toy.

LESSON NUMBER 1: SEEK HELP WHEN YOU NEED IT, AND KEEP SEEKING UNTIL YOU FIND IT

You will always need help with your first doctoral advisee. If I had known then what I know now, I would have contacted my major professor at OSU and sought his help since I could not find the help I needed at LSU. I feel certain that Dr. McCracken would have graciously consented to help me get my first student through the process with considerably less pain for both of us.

CHAPTER 2

LIKE HELL YOU WILL!!

I had the opportunity to work with a young woman who was a staff member on campus. She was married to a man who had recently completed his education in one of the medical fields, and she had worked and supported him while he was in school. After he graduated and started bringing in some money to the family, she had enrolled in a master's program in our School and when she completed this degree, she decided that she wanted to continue toward the completion of her doctorate. She and her husband had two young children during these years, and she was about two-thirds of the way through the coursework component of her doctorate (still working full time on campus), and she came in for her advising appointment (I usually try to do about two of these per semester during the coursework part of the program), and she announced to me that she was resigning from the program. I asked her why and she explained to me that her husband had left her and that with two small children who had lost their father she could not take the time away from them to work on her degree. Therefore, she said, I am going to resign from the program. My next comment came out without really thinking, and it really surprised me a bit. I told her, "Like Hell You Will!! Your children need you to finish this degree now more than ever. Take a semester off, take two if you need them, but after that I better see you back here working on finishing this degree." Was I overstepping my boundaries by saying this? Maybe. Was it out of

Mentoring Doctoral Students in Higher Education:
An International Perspective, pages 5–7.
Copyright © 2025 *Michael F. Burnett*
Published under exclusive licence by Emerald Publishing Limited
ISBN: 979-8-88730-847-0 (PB); 979-8-88730-848-7 (HB); 979-8-88730-849-4 (EPDF)

line? Maybe. All I knew at the time was that a student about whom I cared a great deal with tremendous ability and potential for professional growth if she finished the degree, was going to let a set of circumstances beyond her control wash her out of the program, and I was not willing to accept that.

She did take a semester off. Thankfully, she had family in town, and she arranged for her Mother to care for the children while she finished her courses. We then selected a dissertation topic about which she had a great deal of passion, and she finished her degree well within the allocated time limit. The great news: She met someone, fell in love, and married a man who freely admitted to me when I met him that he knows he got the better deal in their marriage. Some years later, she left LSU (I am sad to say) for a position in the private sector at a considerably higher position and salary.

LESSON NUMBER 2: WHEN YOU FEEL STRONGLY ABOUT SOMETHING, JUST SAY WHAT YOU THINK, EVEN IF IT SEEMS A LITTLE OFF

I know, this could have backfired on me, but because I knew this young woman from having developed a close working relationship with her, I let my instincts take over when I felt that she was threatened. Having worked with well over 150 students spread over the last 40 years, I could count on one hand the number of times I have done this. However, in every case I knew that it was critical.

Oh yes, and not all of them have been positive comments. For example, I agreed to take over working with a student for a faculty member who was leaving LSU. He told her that the University would not allow him to work with her through the completion of her program. Generally, LSU will allow a faculty member who is leaving to have one year to complete a doctoral student in the latter stages of their program. They normally ask for the Department to have someone still at LSU to serve as the student's co-chair. He chose not to share this information with her. He obviously just wanted to move on, which was fine except for one thing. He had another student that was at about the same stage in her program that he chose to keep as an advisee. Unfortunately, the two students were friends, and they talked. It is easy to see why the student he dropped felt abandoned and betrayed when she found out that he had misled her about his ability to continue working with her. She had a very negative attitude toward me and frequently made comments that bordered on openly rude and often stepped over the line of disrespectful. I am still not sure exactly why she was angry with me—whether it was because she just expected me to abandon her the way he did or because she realized that I knew the truth but did not point out to her that he dropped her but kept another student. I think it would have been unprofessional and inappropriate for me to tell her this about her former advisor. She would be on campus for another meeting and would leave and go home to call me for a meeting by telephone apparently because she did not want to meet with me in person, and this was before COVID. Finally, it reached the point that I informed her in writing that the next meeting would be face-to-face; and when we met, I confronted her with the situation which was—For whatever reason you don't trust me, and without trust I cannot get you through this process successfully. I told her that if she did not trust me, she should find someone else with whom to work, but that it would be her decision, because I was not going to drop her as a student. After this, things got a little better, and she did finish her degree, but not without several rougher roads.

CHAPTER 3

THE VALUE OF DETERMINATION AND PERSISTENACE

One of the professors in my doctoral program at Ohio State University (Dr. L. H. Newcomb) told a small group of us who had requested to have lunch with him to "Pick his Brain" said something that I have always remembered and have tried to use as one of my guiding principles in my professional life. He explained to us that many people who complete a Ph.D. develop the attitude that they are somehow better than the rest of the world around them—that they have somehow been blessed from on high. He said that when we graduate, we should be very proud of our achievement because it is a great accomplishment that required a lot of persistence and hard work. However, he admonished us to never forget that completing a doctorate is about 99% perspiration and only 1% inspiration. It does not make you better than other people. It just means that you had an opportunity and worked very hard to take advantage of that opportunity. I cannot help but believe that my Dad (who was very important in my life) could have done this if he had been afforded the opportunity.

Consequently, I have always taken the position that it is inappropriate for me to shove my degree in people's faces. I was an officer in the PTA at my oldest daughter's elementary school for years, and it was not until my second daughter was enrolled in that same school five years later that they found out that I had a doctorate. It was not that I was ashamed of my degree, but rather that I was better able to work with the teachers in the school when they saw me as a parent. Once they knew that I had a doctorate, and especially that my doctorate was in a field of education, they seemed to become intimidated by my degree.

Let's get back to persistence. We had a new student who enrolled in our doctoral program. He was from one of the African countries, and he came here on a Fulbright Scholarship (which is rather prestigious). During his first semester in our program, one of the courses in which he was enrolled was my introductory research course. About mid-way through the course, he approached me after class one evening and asked that I serve as his major professor. I thanked him but told him that due to administrative responsibilities I was going to have to respectfully decline. Another faculty member in our School who was teaching one of the other courses in which this student was enrolled was aggressively trying to get him to select her as his major professor. During the next semester, he was enrolled in my second required research course, and again he came and asked me to accept him as a doctoral advisee. By this time, I had seen the quality of this young man's work, and I must admit (as I did to him) that I was tempted, but again I said no. During the third course in the research sequence of courses, he once again came to me and made an impassioned plea for me to accept him as an advisee. He promised that he would make every effort to take as little of my time as possible and to work very hard and as much as possible on his own. He never said a negative word about my colleague who was recruiting him, but rather he focused his comments on why he needed to work with me. This time I agreed with one stipulation—if at any point he felt that his academic and advising needs would be better met by someone else, he could change with no hard feelings and with no negative repercussions.

This student turned out to be one of the finest students I have ever had the privilege to advise. Any assignment that I gave him was completed with exceptionally high quality and in a very timely manner. In fact, the time it would take him to complete an assignment for me was often stunning. During his last semester of enrollment, he had submitted a paper from his dissertation to a research conference that was meeting in New Orleans. He had listed my name as a co-author on the paper, and we rode together to New Orleans (about a one and one-half hour ride) to present the paper. His presentation had his usual level of excellence, and his paper was selected as the outstanding paper at the conference. On the drive back that evening, we had the time to just visit. He was preparing to return to his home country in Africa and indicated that he wanted to share a couple of things with me. I said OKAY, and he told me this:

1. From the time he arrived here he felt "led" to get me to serve as his major professor,

2. He said that he was going to try three times to get me to accept this role, and that if after three times I still said no he would work with someone else, and
3. He promised himself that if I said yes, whenever I gave him an assignment to complete that he would not sleep until he finished that assignment. He said he kept that promise. This was, of course, why his work was always completed in such a timely manner.

In many ways this made me feel guilty for the times that I know he went for multiple nights without sleep. Had I known what he was doing, I would have strenuously objected, which is, he said, why he never told me until after he was finished.

This student returned to his home country, and a few years later, he applied and was interviewed for an open position we advertised in our School. He would have come for essentially whatever we had been able to offer. However, two of my "enemies" among the faculty worked together (even though they hated each other) to have him declared as unacceptable for the position. Therefore, we were not able to hire him even though he had an extensive publication record, his teaching evaluations were stellar, and he had a strong set of experiences in service to his institution, to the community, and to the profession. When we passed him by, he applied at another university, and based on his vita and his letters of recommendation, they hired him without even requiring that he complete an on-site interview. He quickly became one of that institution's most productive scholars and, several years later, was recruited to apply for a position at a major research university. He was hired there, and after about six years, he was placed in a shadowing program with the university's chief academic officer because they had plans for him in the upper administration of the university. He quickly became an academic dean at this institution and, within the past year this young man moved into a vice-president position at a major research university. I would not be surprised to learn that he was a university president or chancellor in the near future. UNACCEPTABLE???—Right. Talk about narrow-minded and short-sighted and, based on my years of experience in higher education, the conversation must travel through these two people.

LESSON NUMBER 3: WHEN SOMETHING KEEPS COMING BACK TO YOU, THERE IS USUALLY A REASON: BE OPEN TO WHATEVER IT MAY BE

This case that I have just described is an excellent example of the good that can come from being open to persistence. There will, however, be cases where the thing that keeps coming back to you is not so positive. I was working with a young man who just kept making the same mistakes over and over again. He feigned attention when we would meet, but he just would not fix the problems in his study. For example, if I told him that there was an essential correction in one of his objectives, and that he should make the change everywhere the objective appeared throughout the study; he might make the change in the place I marked, but it would be unchanged throughout the rest of the study. One observation that I made about him was that he made revisions by the "Rule of Thirds." If I handed him a set of revisions covering 30 pages in his document, he would make SOME of the revisions in the first third (10 pages or so); a FEW of the revisions in the second third (the next 10 pages or so); and NONE of the revisions in the last third (the last 10 pages or so). Consequently, I was making the same revisions to his document (which was very lengthy) over and over again. This had gone on for more than a year; and finally, I told him that I had given his research my first priority (which I had) for more than a year and that I was going to help another student finish that semester, so his graduation would be postponed—yet again. I told him that he needed to decide if he really wanted to finish this degree and if so, be ready to work in four months. It still was not great, but he did get finished. He had a severe deficiency of persistence, and I am still a little surprised that he finally did finish.

CHAPTER 4

THE RIGHT TOPIC

A lesson that I always try to drive home in my introductory research methods course is that the most important criteria for selection of a research problem is the importance and significance of the topic. I do believe that, but there are many different important and significant topics from which students can choose. I had the pleasure of working with a young woman who was extremely bright and had a "Get it Done" philosophy about most things in her life. She was very doubtful about her ability to pass the required statistics courses, which is not an uncommon situation among students in our program. However, most students put off taking the statistics courses as a reaction to this anxiety. This student said that she was going to take statistics first. She reasoned that "If I can't pass statistics, then why waste the time and money to do the other courses in the program." Well, she made an "A" in both of her required statistics courses. When she passed her general examination and moved into the dissertation phase of the program, she was stuck (Top Dead Center!).

At about the same time that she was struggling with this dilemma, I was being asked to assume the role as major professor for another student in the program. This was a lady whose major professor had moved into an administrative position and just did not have the time to work with her. In his new role, he had the need for a study to be conducted, and he had directed her to do the research. He also indicated that his new office would pay the expenses of the research; so, she had her dissertation research funded. We immediately started meeting on a weekly basis, and I quickly picked up on the fact that she was making very little progress on her research proposal. Finally, one day at our regular meeting, I asked her what was going on. She was a little reluctant to speak openly about the problem, but I persisted; and, finally she told me that this was the most boring topic she could even imagine. She said, "Every time I sit down to work on this proposal, I fall asleep." My next logical question was simply, then why are you doing this study? She said that her former major professor had directed her to do the study because he needed the information. I next asked if she knew what she wanted to study. She said yes and told me what she really wanted to do. My comment was, "Then do it." Her next question was, "But what about being directed to do this study?" To this I said, "There's a new sheriff in town, and it is me."

I know that many scholars take the position that if we are to move the body of knowledge forward, faculty researchers should have a clear focus and should require their doctoral students to conduct their dissertation research in that focus area. In contrast, my position has always been that the students should choose an area for their research for which they have a passion, because it will/should be the focus of their research in their scholarly career. Therefore, this second student moved to her topic of research interest and embarked on an outstanding study which was her area of focus when she entered the role of faculty researcher.

You might think that I just left the second student's former major professor in a lurch since he now had no one to conduct the study he needed in his new role. Not true—as the first student and I brainstormed topics, I shared with her the available funding to do the study that the second student had been previously assigned to complete. This piqued her interest and soon she was completely immersed in the literature for this area. She embraced the study and went far beyond the minimum requirements to complete an outstanding dissertation. Everybody was happy with the outcomes. The second student was happy because she got to do the study she wanted to complete; The first student was happy because she found a topic for which she had a passion; The second student's former advisor was happy because he got the study he needed and then some; and I was happy because I got to work with two outstanding doctoral students who were excited about the work they were doing.

LESSON NUMBER 4: ENCOURAGE AND HELP STUDENTS TO FIND A RESEARCH TOPIC FOR WHICH THEY HAVE A PASSION: THE PROCESS WILL PROCEED MORE SMOOTHLY AND THE OUTCOMES WILL BE BETTER

I am not completely naive. I know that things will not always run this smoothly but think about how things might have gone without these changes. Besides: the second student did not really need the funding for her dissertation research and the first student did.

CHAPTER 5

MOTIVATED!

Motivation is probably the most important quality that influences a person's performance in virtually any area. A person who is a high achiever in school is usually a person who is highly motivated to do well in school. A person who is a high achiever at work is typically a person who is highly motivated to be successful in their job. Many different things may be the source of motivation for a person. For example, a student who is from a financially poor family in a low-income neighborhood and has some athletic talent may be motivated to become an outstanding athlete to escape from poverty. That person may work hard and become the best running back in college football in the United States. He may then sign a very lucrative contract to play professional football. He has, thus escaped the poverty in which he lived as a child. Motivation may be pushed on someone. "Your grandfather was a doctor, your Father was a doctor, and you ARE going to be a doctor." Some people are susceptible to this type of pressure motivation and others are not. Ultimately for a person to be successful AND happy in their profession, they must internalize the motivation.

For example, my dad was motivated to accept a job with the U. S. Postal Service because he was out of work and needed to provide a living for his family. He became very good at what he did, but he would never accept promotions because he hated the work that he did and did not want to be part of the management structure of an organization that, in his opinion and experience, cared nothing for its employees. His motivations were clear and pure but unfortunate because he never found his way out of that organization until retirement. After retirement he was able to devote himself to something for which he had a passion but think of the years lost.

From the time I entered school, my mother pushed me very hard (sometimes too hard I think) to do well in school. If I brought home a report card (Yes, they were cards back then), and I had seven "A's" and one "B." she just breezed right past those seven "A's" and wanted to know why I made that "B." Somewhere along the way in my life, I internalized that motivation to do well in school. It could not have been just pressure, because I tend to be resistant to most forms of pressure. In fact, I tend to push back. I graduated seventh in my high school graduating class of 306 students. I graduated from college with highest Latin honors at Clemson University, etc. I do know a little about the effects that motivation can have on a person, especially in the area of academic achievement.

There was a young woman in our program who had been enrolled for several years and just seemed to be cruising along—sort of like a driver who is not exiting from the Interstate, but also not in enough of a hurry to stay much above the minimum speed. I had taught her in three courses and found her to be a competent student but not really an achiever. She was one of the students who had asked my administrator to be her major professor, and I was formally her Co-Chair, but she never asked for appointments, and she never really seemed to make any progress toward her degree. One afternoon in the early Summer, while I was serving as the associate dean of the College, she called and asked for an appointment. When she came to my office, she made a very earnest request that she wanted to finish her degree by the following December and asked me to help her achieve this goal. I had several students with whom I was working, but only one of these was "Deep" into the dissertation process. Most of the others were still taking courses; and the one in the dissertation stage was clearly not serious about getting finished because he would not pay attention to my advice and direction. Consequently, I felt very confident that if she really wanted to do this, I could help her make it happen.

Over the course of the next four months, this young woman became one of the most diligent and hard-working students with whom I had ever worked. We met in the beginning once each week, and as she progressed in her study, this grew to twice per week and eventually three times per week. She never missed a meeting; she was never late for meetings; she never failed to complete the assignments I had given her, at least as well as she understood them; and she never complained. She came to me with a clear idea of what she wanted to study for her dissertation research, and she very quickly had an approved proposal. These circumstances are a recipe for success; and that is exactly what she found—success. Remember, completing a doctorate is 99% perspiration and only 1% inspiration; and she definitely put in the "perspiration." I could write another two pages about the scholarly and professional successes she experienced over the next three years after finishing her degree; but if I told you too much I might as well print her name in the book. Suffice it to say that when she found the motivation, she showed that she was truly a person of exceptional ability. We just had not seen it before.

LESSON NUMBER 5: LEARN TO RECOGNIZE TRUE MOTIVATION BECAUSE THERE IS NO QUALITY THAT GIVES A MORE DIRECT PATH TO SUCCESS FOR YOU AND YOUR STUDENT

Like my dad, and me as a child, motivation can come from many different sources. I worked with a doctoral student many years ago whose motivation was simply that he could not return to his home country without the degree. He told me that it did not really matter in which major he completed his degree, he just had to complete it. Otherwise, he would go home in disgrace and his career prospects would be dismal. I have worked with other students who had the completion of a Ph.D. as a personal life goal. One of them graduated with her doctorate and retired the next semester. I have spoken with her recently and she is loving being Dr. Grandma. Another student retired and graduated the next semester.

I have worked with a number of students who had no clear motivation and just seemed to float along in the program. Some of these may actually graduate at some point, but even when they do, they typically do not participate in commencement, and I usually do not hear from them again.

CHAPTER 6

BEWARE OF MANIPULATOR

For many years now, I have been of the opinion that we should handle teaching evaluations using the "Olympic scoring" approach. In many of the events at the Olympics that use judges, such as Gymnastics, diving, and Figure Skating, a process is (or at least has been) used such that the highest and lowest scores are dropped, and the remaining scores are used for determining an individual's final score in the event. I believe that in any course, there will be some students (generally a small percentage—about 5 to no more than 10%) who are of the opinion that you can do nothing wrong (at least that is what they say on the evaluations); and I assure you they are wrong. About the same number (5 to 10%) are of the opinion that you can do nothing right; and they are wrong also. If we threw out the highest 5% of the evaluations and the lowest 5% of the evaluations, we would have a much better representation of how well the teacher is actually doing in their instructional role. In your role as a doctoral advisor, you will also have these same groups represented. The ones who think you can do nothing right will take care of themselves if you make it easy for them to change major professors. However, the ones who will tell you that you are perfect are the ones you need to guard against. I am not talking about the nice things that students say about you in the acknowledgement section of their dissertation. At that point, it is too late for their flattery to really impact the amount of effort that you are willing to expend

Mentoring Doctoral Students in Higher Education:
An International Perspective, pages 19–23.
Copyright © 2025 *Michael F. Burnett*
Published under exclusive licence by Emerald Publishing Limited
ISBN: 979-8-88730-847-0 (PB); 979-8-88730-848-7 (HB); 979-8-88730-849-4 (EPDF)

on them. Neither can it impact you spending the amount of time necessary to help your student be successful.

What I am talking about is the person who "Pours on the butter and syrup" to get you to do their work for them or to use your influence to allow them to avoid the normal and reasonable expectations required for their degree completion. I have seen this happen all too often in my years at LSU, and even had it tried on me a few times.

One specific example of this phenomenon happened when an exceptionally lazy student enrolled in the program decided that he would try to avoid a lot of his work by flattering his major professor, who also happened to be the head of the program at the time. He spent hours in her office telling her how wonderful she was, and she responded by sitting with him while "He" did his assignments for the courses in which he was enrolled. When it came time for his general examination, the student followed very much the same process. He wrote the examinations from the other members of his committee (including mine) sitting in her office and interacting with her frequently, mostly about the content of the questions he had been assigned to answer. Even with this assistance, his responses were less than stellar, and he was very late getting them distributed to the members of his committee. The policy in our School at that time was that students SHOULD distribute the complete set of responses to the members of the graduate advisory committee two weeks before the oral portion of the examination, and that they MUST distribute them at least one week before the oral. His oral was scheduled on a Monday morning, and he distributed his written responses to the committee members late the Friday afternoon before. This meant that we had only the weekend to review the exam responses. Additionally, the person who was assigned as his Dean's Representative was not in her office on that Friday afternoon, and she, therefore, did not receive her copy of the responses until she walked into the exam room. Since the exam was in the early morning, she did not go to her office before coming to the exam, so her copy was still in her office mailbox. When she asked that the meeting be postponed until she had the opportunity to review his written exam, his major professor literally verbally assaulted the Dean's Representative. This young woman was a first-year assistant professor in another department, but nevertheless a beginning assistant professor and easily intimidated. One of the things that I have most regretted in my career is that I did not "Dig my heels in" and demand that the exam be postponed. She (the major professor) WAS my direct supervisor, and I allowed myself to be intimidated by this fact, even though I knew what I should have done. The student wrote his dissertation in much the same way as he had his general examination—sitting in his major professor's office with her either doing the writing or dictating the information to him. I do not know if she ever figured out what he was doing, but everybody else in the School (faculty, staff, and students) knew it.

A similar situation occurred a couple of years later with another doctoral student and the same major professor. This was a woman who was employed as an instructor at one of the small state universities in Louisiana. She could easily have been referred to as the "Queen of Excuses." No matter what was due, she had some type of excuse (usually medical) for being late. She apparently had family members who were in the medical profession, and she found it very easy to acquire a medical excuse. Every time she had one of my final exams, she was unable to take the exam because of a rather extreme medical condition (each one different from the one before). In my second course in the sequence of research courses required of doctoral students, she was not at the exam, and came in the next day with medical documentation that whenever she had an exam scheduled, she experienced stress blindness. I am not a medical doctor, and I presume that such a condition does exist, but she did not have the same problem at the final exam in my first course, and no other faculty member had heard this specific excuse. In every case, she persuaded her major professor to validate her excuse, and to use her influence to prevent the committee from holding her accountable. This student did not actually function in the same way as the one discussed previously when it came to writing the dissertation. In fact, as was discovered some time later (unfortunately after the degree had been completed, but thankfully, without me) that she had hired someone to write her dissertation for her. After she was awarded her degree, she moved from an instructor position into a tenure-track assistant professor position at her university. However, a few years later she was fired by this university for poor performance in all aspects of her job. Poetic Justice or karma or whatever you want to call it does exist, I guess.

Our School had always used the admission requirements established by the Graduate School for admission to our doctoral program. For a period of one year, the Graduate School eliminated the requirement of completing the Graduate Record Examination (GRE) with a minimum score as one of the admission requirements. During this time, a small group of students gained admission to the doctoral program who should not have been there. One of these was a very attractive young woman. After she was admitted, she immediately began working on her strategy for completing the program.

One of the faculty members in our School at the time was an exceptional female faculty member who was also African American. This lady was one of, if not the best teacher in the school and a true pioneer in distance learning in the State of Louisiana. This student was also African American. Her first attempt at manipulation was to go into this faculty members office, sit on the edge of her desk, and say, "What's happening sister?" The faculty member (who is still one of my very dear friends) told her, "I am NOT your sister, and get your butt off of my desk." Her next round of manipulation efforts were through passive sexual advances. She would go into a male faculty member's office wearing a very tight, low-cut top and lean over the desk on a pretense of asking a question about something on a paper. Unfortunately, for her this action became one of the main topics of discussion among the faculty, both male and female, essentially negating its potential influence. Eventually, when she realized that if she was going to get a degree, she might have to actually work for it, she resigned from the program and left. It was her best move.

Manipulators will use a lot of things, many of which I have seen in operation, but the worst of them (in my opinion) is threats. A man entered our program and very quickly showed himself to be a very mediocre student at best (due primarily to laziness—in my opinion). At that time, the Graduate School required that all doctoral students have a program of studies approved by their doctoral advisory committee early in the program. He immediately started looking for ways to cut corners. He came and discussed with me what my research and statistics course expectations would be IF he chose to put me on his committee. He apparently did not like what I said, because I was systematically omitted from his committee. I was pleased with his decision, but as you will see it did not keep me out of the line of fire. In fact, he had completed one master's level statistics course at a small college during his master's program, and since I told him I was not willing to allow him to use this one course to satisfy the requirement for his doctoral statistics (typically two doctoral level statistics courses), he did not want me to bring this position to his doctoral advisory committee. My position was based on the inappropriateness of substituting three hours of master's level statistics credit for eight hours of doctoral level statistics credit.

Please take note that I was NOT a member of his committee. However, when he was not successful in completing his general examination, he filed a lawsuit against the University, our College, our School, and me specifically for having prejudicially influenced his committee to make the decision not to pass him. They did not vote to fail, but rather told him that they wanted him to complete some additional assignments before they were willing to sign the forms indicating that he had passed. Over the next six months, he told people in the School that he was a member of an elite military group that was highly trained in the art of killing. One of the members of the committee had a nervous breakdown and retired early citing veiled threats from this man as the main reason for his breakdown. Two of my very close friends that were members of the committee noted that they received multiple veiled threats on their safety, and one member of the committee died in a hiking accident under suspicious circumstances. I was harassed until, thankfully, the University's lawyers gave me strict instructions that I was not to interact personally with him under any circumstances and that any written communication had to be routed through them before it was sent to him. This was a welcome restriction. I spent literally hundreds of hours preparing reports addressing the untrue accusations and charges that he leveled against our program in general and me in specific.

Ultimately it was discovered that he had broken university policies during his time here, and the administration of the University told him that if he went away, they would not bring charges against him. Actually, he broke a rule that you simply cannot break in a university. In fact, one of the administrators with whom I interacted during this investigation characterized this as "The Holy Grail of Academia." He had for a few years been teaching an undergraduate course on an adjunct basis for another program on campus. He signed up for the course he was teaching and assigned himself an "A" in the course to pad his academic background in preparation for transferring to that program for his doctorate.

LESSON NUMBER 6: BE WARY WHENEVER A STUDENT TAKES ACTIONS THAT ARE DESIGNED TO AVOID FULFILLING THEIR OBLIGATIONS AS A STUDENT. THIS PERSON MAY BE A MANIPULATOR

Manipulators use many different approaches including flattery, pitting you against another faculty member, threats, or even sexual advances. Just because a student says something to you that is designed to flatter, does not mean they are a manipulator. What you need to look for is efforts to get out of work or, especially, to get you to do their work for them. I do "hold their feet to the fire" when it comes to my students doing their academic work at a very high level of quality. My rule is that "It doesn't go to the committee until **I** say it goes to the committee." As I have mentioned earlier, I tell every one of my students this rule and I tell them that if they cannot accept this, they should find someone else to chair their committee.

CHAPTER 7

HONESTY

I have long been known among the faculty, staff, and students as a "soft touch." When students need an extension or help with assignments, I rarely say no. I am of the belief that 95% of the time when students ask for consideration or help, it is legitimate and for a worthy reason. I would rather be taken advantage of 5% of the time than worsening a difficult situation unjustly for the other 95%. Therefore, if a student comes to me and says that their child was very ill and they were unable to complete an assignment so they need extra time, I will grant them that time. Now, if I learn later that this person does not have a child, I will confront them with their lie and explain that they need not ask me for this type of consideration again. Many people interpret that being a "soft touch" means that I am easy to take advantage of, and I guess to a point that is true. However, when you pass that point, it is very difficult to return. When it comes to my doctoral advisees, there is one thing that I demand absolutely, and that is honesty. A student can come to me and tell me that he did not get his work done because he took his family on a weekend vacation, and that is okay. I may caution him on the impact that this will have on his progress if he does not get busy. However, as long as the student is honest, we can work through it.

I was working with a young woman who had a topic about which she was passionately motivated to conduct her dissertation research. This is always a great

Mentoring Doctoral Students in Higher Education:
An International Perspective, pages 25–27.
Copyright © 2025 *Michael F. Burnett*
Published under exclusive licence by Emerald Publishing Limited
ISBN: 979-8-88730-847-0 (PB); 979-8-88730-848-7 (HB); 979-8-88730-849-4 (EPDF)

situation, because generally, you do not have to push the student—they will push themselves. This student was a bit impatient, and as she searched for instruments in the literature to measure the constructs she wanted to measure, she found that there were lots of instruments, but they were all copyrighted and were relatively expensive to purchase. So, she located a couple of instruments that were relatively obscure (still copyrighted) and indicated in her proposal draft (it had not gotten past me at this point, thankfully) that they were public domain instruments available to anyone who wanted to use them.

As I reviewed the draft of the proposal, I became suspicious about the availability of the instruments. Consequently, when we next met a couple of days later, I asked her about the instruments. She looked me straight in the eyes and lied to me about the instruments (of which I had found the sources). I revealed to her what I had discovered and told her that she needed to find another major professor. If I cannot trust my students to be honest with me, I do not need to be working with them. In the 43 years that I have been working with doctoral students, I have heard just about every reason imaginable for a student failing to get their work completed. Some of these are:

1. Sick children,
2. Family reunions,
3. Marital separation,
4. Marital reconciliation,
5. Personal illness,
6. Vacation,
7. Just tired,
8. Automobile accidents,
9. Sick pet,
10. Death in the family,
11. Wife and child disappeared,
12. Etc.

As long as they are honest with me, I can deal with whatever they tell me.

This young woman did not break into tears, and she was not angry. In fact, she just seemed to be embarrassed. I explained to her that what she had done was plagiarism, and that if it had gotten into her dissertation, the university would very likely have revoked her degree—no matter how many years it had been since it was awarded. However, as I explained to her, the dishonesty with me was what I considered the gravest error she committed in this situation. I explained that, in all likelihood, her plagiarism would be discovered, and that I would never knowingly allow a student to commit plagiarism in their dissertation. She wanted to know what it would take to persuade me to continue as her major professor. We had another meeting scheduled in about three days, and I told her that she should keep that meeting. Between now and then she should think long and hard about whether or not she really wanted me to continue as her advisor. I told her that she should make a list of the reasons that she wanted me to continue as her chair and a list of reasons that I SHOULD continue as her chair. In that same time period, I would think long and hard about whether or not I was even willing to consider continuing as her chair. When next we met, she said that she DID want me to continue as her chair, and she provided a list of reasons that she wanted this. However, she said that she could not give me a single reason that I should continue. She accepted full responsibility for her actions, and she promised that she would never lie to me again.

I did continue as her chair, and she did get her degree. Did she take advantage of me? Maybe, but I checked everything she submitted to me after that with a fine-toothed comb, and, to the best of my knowledge, she kept her word.

LESSON NUMBER 7: IF YOU LOOK FOR ONE CHARACTERISTIC OF YOUR RELATIONSHIP WITH YOUR STUDENTS THAT IS MOST IMPORTANT, THAT CHARACTERISTIC IS HONESTY

Am I really suggesting that my students have never lied to me? Of course not! I am not THAT naïve. However, I do emphasize the importance of honesty in our relationship, and I believe that most of them have been honest with me throughout the process. Many of these have become very close friends AFTER they finished their degree

CHAPTER 8

EXPERIENCES

When I was enrolled in my doctoral program, I was a bit bothered by the fact that I was just one of so many graduate assistants in the program. When I was working on my master's degree at Clemson University, I was the ONLY graduate assistant in the program. Consequently, I was called on by every faculty member to help with everything with which they needed assistance. At OSU, I had my assignments for my research grant, and basically no one bothered me beyond this. At some point about two years into my program, I decided to ask about supplemental experiences. At this point, Dr. Warmbrod was the head of the Department, and he asked what type of experiences I wanted. Boy did this open the door. During my third year at OSU, I accompanied three different faculty members (including Dr. Warmbrod) on student teacher visits and actually got the chance to conduct sessions under Dr. Warmbrod's supervision. In case I have not mentioned earlier, Dr. Warmbrod is probably—No DEFINITELY—the best master teacher I have ever encountered in my life. Imagine the opportunity to ride with him an hour and a half to the school where the student was assigned, observing him conduct a student teaching evaluation, and then getting to spend an hour riding back with him after the fact. I got to do the same thing with Dr. Ralph Bender. Dr. Bender was a member of the first national officer team of the FFA (Future Farmers of America) and was the head of the Department for more than 30 years. Some of my most valuable experiences took place outside of the classroom.

I have a colleague at LSU who is retired (and has been for quite some time) who is one of the very finest people I have ever had the privilege to know. After his retirement he continued to teach courses for our School for several years. However, at his age managing the technology associated with the teaching process at LSU was somewhat of a problem for him. Consequently, I assigned a graduate assistant for a portion of their work assignment to assist him with teaching his course. I only had the chance to do this once, because after the word got out about the quality and value of the experience that the student received while working closely with him, I had doctoral students literally "Lined up" to fill this role. One former student reported to me that this experience had the most significant impact of all his educational experiences on his success as a beginning faculty member at another university. In all, about six students had the opportunity to serve as his teaching assistant which was at least one each time he taught a course for us. Eventually, he made the decision to discontinue his teaching because it was just too difficult for him to drive after dark. He has, however, continued to serve on doctoral students' committees. He has remarked to me that he feels like students only get about 50% of what they used to get from him as a committee member. What I tell him is that first I do not agree, but if that is true, his 50% is more than most people's 100%. Therefore, I am still pushing for the wonderful experiences that he provides for my students by being part of their committees (and he is currently a member of most of my students' committees).

A young woman who was a doctoral student in our program called one day and scheduled an appointment to meet with me. When she came into my office and sat down, she told me that she would not take much of my time; that she just wanted to let me know that she was resigning from the program. I asked why, and she said that all she did in the program was take courses, memorize the information in the course, write it down on the final exam, and then start another semester doing the same thing. By this time, I was in the other program that was created when the reorganization occurred; so, I was not her Director/Department Head at that point. Additionally, I was not her major professor at that time, so I asked her "Why are you telling this to me? Shouldn't you be telling your Director that you are resigning from his program? She said that the reason she came to me was that my courses (she had completed three) were the only ones in which she felt challenged. I asked if that was what she wanted—to be challenged—and she said yes. I said that if she wanted a challenge, I could arrange that. She moved to our program, I agreed to serve as her major professor, and I set her up with a series of experiences (mostly out of class) designed to challenge her. First, I visited with her enough to know where her greatest interests lay. I then identified a colleague with exceptional expertise in those areas and arranged one-on-one sessions on those topics. These sessions were with retired colleagues, so they had the time and the desire, and the student reaped the benefits. Oh, by the way, she finished her degree, got married to her high school sweetheart, and now has three absolutely gorgeous children.

LESSON NUMBER 8: REMEMBER THAT NOT ALL VALUABLE EXPERIENCES OCCUR IN A CLASSROOM. DON'T JUST ALLOW STUDENTS TO GAIN THESE EXPERIENCES—ENCOURAGE THEM TO DO SO

When I came to LSU, one of the first assignments given to me was supervising student teachers. I arrived here on August 1, 1980, and in the spring semester I had eight student teachers to supervise. Imagine where I would have been without those supplemental experiences that I had during my last year at OSU. Instead of being prepared to "Hit the ground running" I would have probably started with a stutter step. Help your students to be prepared for their first job in higher education by helping them to get the experiences they need to be ready for the job duties they are likely to encounter.

CHAPTER 9

IS DESIRE ENOUGH?

There is an old proverb, "If wishes were horses, beggars would ride." As I understand, this was first recorded in the 17th century; and to me its application to the topic of this book is embedded in the question, "Is desire enough?" Completing a Ph.D. requires a lot of sacrifices of many and varied types. When I decided that I wanted to complete a doctorate, there were a lot of decisions with which I had to wrestle:

1. Would I go to Ohio State which was reputed to be the "best" Ag Ed program in the country at the time?
2. Would I wait for Clemson to gain approval on the program they were pursuing at the time? (It was literally years before this program gained approval.)
3. Would I enroll in a program in a different area to stay close to home?
4. Would I quit a stable job for a graduate assistant salary of $450.00 per month (about one third of my current salary)?
5. Would I move to a part of the country I had never even visited?
6. Would I enroll in a program that might be over my head?
7. Would I uproot my wife from her family and move her into the Midwest?

I could go on and on with the questions that ran through my mind while I was preparing to go to Ohio State to work on my doctorate. I was moving 650 miles—just think about those people who are moving halfway around the world. I had the desire, but it took more than just desire. I had to make sacrifices, and I had to change my system of priorities, at least for a while. I have mentioned before that a close friend and colleague at LSU would regularly tell new doctoral students that at some point, completing this degree will become the most important thing in your life or you will NOT complete the degree.

During my time at LSU, I have encountered a lot of students who had a deep passionate desire to have a doctorate. However, wanting a doctorate and completing a doctorate CAN be two very different things. I had a friend in my baccalaureate program who had an unmatched wit. One of his witticisms that I have heard him say on a number of occasions to individuals who stated emphatically that they were going to have something (say a fancy sports car)—go ahead and have one, it is cheaper than buying it. I have also mentioned before in this book that Dr. Newcomb (one of my professors at Ohio State) reminded us that completing a doctorate was 99% perspiration and only 1% inspiration. This is why I have taken the position that I have on this issue—Is desire enough?

When teaching students in my research design course about the concept of interaction between independent variables in a study, I always approach it from the standpoint that if someone asks you which level of the primary independent variable works better, if your answer is "It Depends" then you have an interaction between the variables. For example, if I am studying the impact of type of feedback on assignments (written versus verbal) and I find that verbal feedback tends to work better for females and written feedback tends to work better for males, then if you are asked the question which type of feedback works better, you would have to say it depends. In this case it depends on whether the student is male or female. There is an interaction between type of feedback and gender of student.

So, is desire enough? I keep flitting around the question but why not take a position. Here it is—NO! desire is not enough, but desire IS a critical component. Personally, I believe that the 1% that Dr. Newcomb talked about could easily be called desire. A person must be inspired enough to want the degree with a passionate desire. So, what about the other 99%. Let me tell you about a few students who had the desire but were not Ph.D. material by most people's definitions.

A young man entered our program with relatively weak credentials in the area of standardized test scores. His scores were especially weak in the quantitative portion of the test. Needless to say, he was a bit intimidated by the fact that he had to complete eight semester credit hours of doctoral level statistics coursework. He entered the first statistics course and learned right away that he really might be in over his head. So, what did he do? Here is where the perspiration kicked in. He went to visit with the statistics professor (thankfully, we had at that time a man teaching the required statistics courses that was not only a good teacher but also a good person). Based on the meeting, he dropped the course and immediately scheduled a master's level statistics course. It had been more than 10 years since he completed his master's degree, and he did this for a refresher. He did fairly well (but not great) in this course, so when he re-enrolled in his first doctoral statistics course the next semester, he hired a tutor. At his request, he and I also scheduled a weekly meeting to discuss the issues addressed that week in his statistics course. Most of the time, this meeting was not as much about statistics as it was about building a little self-confidence in him. He got through his required statistics courses and while his grades were not "A's" they WERE "B's" and he knew his content well enough to successfully analyze and report his dissertation data. Some people might have said he was not Ph.D. material, but he has a doctorate today and is a highly successful professional at the university where he wanted to work.

Another young man had been a student in our School's master's program and after he completed his M.S. degree, he began seeking admission to the doctoral program. It took several attempts, but he finally convinced the School's graduate admission committee to approve his application so that he could have a chance to get his Ph.D. This young man was very strategic in designing his doctoral program of studies and worked to select the courses that would provide him with the most beneficial information in achieving his career goals. I could tell that he worked hard, but I really did not have a clear understanding of his work ethic until he passed his general examination and started work on his dissertation. This student had completed his baccalaureate degree at one of the smaller state-supported universities in Louisiana. In fact, he began his freshman year enrolled in multiple remedial courses because of deficiencies in his standardized test scores. His freshman remedial English professor stood in front of the room during the first class session of the course and announced to the class that no one who started in this course has ever completed a college degree (at least this is what the student shared with me). I do not know if this comment lit a fire in him or what. However, I DO know that I have never worked with a more organized student in my career. He used every course project in his three required research courses to move toward the development of an approvable dissertation proposal. Soon after his general examination, he was moving deliberately into his research. He established an ambitious timeline for himself and stayed ahead of every point on that timeline. We had regular meetings and he NEVER missed one of those meetings. In fact, he was never even late for one of those meetings. He wasn't just there, he had completed all of the assignments from our previous meeting. He DID have small children and his spouse was also employed in a full-time professional position. I have no doubt that this young man sacrificed many hours of sleep, time with his children, and hours of annual leave to his desire of completing a Ph.D. There is your 99% perspiration.

LESSON NUMBER 9: DESIRE ALONE MAY NOT BE ENOUGH, BUT TRUE PASSIONATE DESIRE WILL CAUSE STUDENTS TO ADD THE OTHER 99% PERSPIRATION NEEDED TO REACH THE GOAL OF EARNING A PH.D.

I could tell you about a dozen other students with similar stories. In the late 1990s our program went through an in-depth program review that included both an internal committee and a group of faculty members from other universities. We fared very well in the review, and at the exit interview where the review team presented their findings to the administration of the University with me as the Director of School in attendance, the Provost made an announcement that was a bit of a surprise to everyone in the room except me. He said that over the past few weeks, he had conducted a series of interviews with faculty from around the university who had served as Dean's Representatives on doctoral committees in our School within the past few years. He said that he was unable to find a single one of these Dean's Representatives who was less than complimentary (and many of them effusive) about the performance of our students and the rigor of our process. He then went on to say that while it is true that our School tends to admit students who are weaker on their academic credentials (especially their standardized test scores), we seem to get outstanding performance from these students. I had known this man who was our Provost at the time for a long time, and I am certain that he did not really mean this as a compliment. However, I can think of NO greater compliment he could have given us. Is Desire Enough?—If it is the right kind of desire and it has the right kind of direction it will usually lead to the desired outcome. Oh, by the way, the reason his announcement was NOT a surprise to me is that some of the Dean's Representatives were friends, and they had called and asked me "What is going on in your School?" They then told me about the call they received and the questions they were asked. My only comment to them was that I hope they told the truth.

CHAPTER 10

PLAGIARISM—OH MY!!

In the original version of the movie *The Wizard of Oz*, as Dorothy, the Tin Woodman, and the Scarecrow enter the dark forest, they become fearful of the dangerous creatures that live in the forest. They start chanting, Lions and Tigers and Bears—Oh My! Over and over again. In the world of academia, plagiarism, in its various forms, might be considered these dangerous creatures. Plagiarism is considered to be one of the most serious forms of academic dishonesty. The Merriam-Webster dictionary defines plagiarize as:

> to steal and pass off (the ideas or words of another) as one's own : use (another's production) without crediting the source. (Merriam-Webster,

If you asked 100 different university faculty to define plagiarism, you would get about 50 different variations of the definition. One of the greatest difficulties is the part of plagiarism that involves stealing another person's ideas. It is very difficult to prove that someone else did not have the same ideas. However, when someone takes another individual's written words and takes credit for them as their own, this is much easier to prove. A question that has often come to my mind about plagiarism is "Is unintentional plagiarism still plagiarism?" At least according to the Dean of Students Office at LSU, the answer is Yes!.

Mentoring Doctoral Students in Higher Education:
An International Perspective, pages 37–41.
Copyright © 2025 *Michael F. Burnett*
Published under exclusive licence by Emerald Publishing Limited
ISBN: 979-8-88730-847-0 (PB); 979-8-88730-848-7 (HB); 979-8-88730-849-4 (EPDF)

Other than minor incidences on class papers, the first real encounter I had with plagiarism at LSU was a doctoral student on whose doctoral advisory committee I served as a member. This student was in another department and in another college, but I had been asked to serve as a member of the committee. She had been finished with her degree for a couple of years when a former student in our School was told that someone else had completed a study that was very similar to the one she had done about ten years earlier. Out of curiosity, she checked the dissertation out of the library (She was a faculty member and faculty could check out University copies of dissertations at that time.). As she read through the study, she found some very disturbing similarities to her study. In fact, she discovered that a large percentage of her Review of Related Literature had been copied in this study verbatim. She notified the Graduate School of the alleged plagiarism and the investigation started.

The Graduate School contracted with an independent editor to analyze the two studies and identify all the cases of plagiarism in the second study. Once this was completed, the student was notified of the findings, and she received the following mandate:

1. Review the report which identified in detail every incidence of plagiarism in her dissertation,
2. Revise her dissertation to meet the requirements of academic integrity, and
3. Re-submit her dissertation, free from plagiarism to the University for satisfying the academic requirements for her Ph.D.

She said that her dissertation would stand exactly as it was originally submitted, and that she would not change a single word. The University then revoked her doctorate! Yes, I have the dubious distinction of being a doctoral advisory committee member of the only Ph.D. in LSU history to be revoked. In my defense, it was not my content area, and consequently, I did not really know the literature in that area very well. Additionally, the original author had been a very good writer, so there were very few needed revisions in the document's wording.

Well, of course, the student sued the University, and all the committee members had to be deposed, and we went through several interviews regarding our role on the committee for the study with the alleged plagiarism. Ultimately, the outcome was that she dropped her lawsuit, and she probably still works (unless she is retired) without a doctorate. My GUESS would be that when her lawyer learned of the offer the University made to just revise the document and re-submit it, he probably advised her that she was wasting her time (and money).

In my opinion, this is plagiarism in its purest form. She simply lifted sections from another person's document and inserted them into her document and claimed that she was the one who wrote them. Nowhere was the original author given credit for the work.

Another young woman in our doctoral program got entangled in self-plagiarism. Some people look at this and say, "How is this possible?" If they were my ideas originally, how can I steal my own ideas? Self-plagiarism can be defined as follows:

> In short, self-plagiarism is any attempt to take any of your own previously published text, papers, or research results and make it appear brand new. (https://www.aje.com/arc/self-plagiarism-how-to-define-it-and-why-to-avoid-it/)

Essentially, what this student did was to submit the exact same document for a project in two different courses in which she was enrolled in the same semester. One of the faculty members involved had already graded the paper and assigned the student a grade of "A" on the project and in the course. However, the second faculty member had discussed with the first faculty member, and they compared notes (and papers). When he realized that what she submitted to him was the same identical paper, he charged her with plagiarism. The Dean of Student's Office found her guilty, and she was required to be separated from the program for one semester. After this time, she was re-admitted and allowed to continue in her doctoral program. However, she never really recovered and shortly after she returned to the program, she resigned and left the program permanently.

Another encounter with plagiarism occurred when a young man was applying for admission to the program. I noticed that he had been dropped from the Graduate School after he made a 2.00 GPA the previous semester. Actually, he was enrolled in two courses, and he made an "A" in one of them and an "F" in the other. Anytime a student at LSU achieves less than a 2.55 GPA in a semester, the Graduate School has the option to drop them. However, this is generally what is referred to as a "Soft drop." This simply means that with a letter of petition from a Department, they can be re-admitted. A "Hard drop" is one from which the student cannot re-admitted without proof of extreme extenuating circumstances or a very strong letter of support from the department to which he is applying. Eventually, I learned from the professor who assigned him a grade of "F" that he had plagiarized a copyrighted document in his project for her class. In fact, he had simply copied a document from the Internet and submitted it AS his project for her course. However, she did NOT report him to the Dean of Students Office; therefore, he escaped with nothing more than one bad grade on his transcript for which he could fabricate any kind of story he liked as an explanation. He was NOT admitted to our School.

For the most part, I have NO sympathy for students who plagiarize other people's work. However, there was one case about which I did and still do feel very badly. A young woman in our program submitted her proposal to her doctoral advisory committee for approval. I was a member of her committee, but I was not her major professor. One of the citations in her proposal was from a Wikipedia site, and her committee strongly insisted that she remove this citation since they did not consider it a scholarly source. Her proposal was approved, and about six months later when she brought her dissertation draft to her committee members, she HAD removed the Wikipedia information and citation from her dissertation. HOWEVER, exactly two sentences had wrapped to the previous page in such a way that they were inadvertently left in the document, but the citation was removed both as a textual citation AND from the reference list.

When her document was distributed to the members of her doctoral advisory committee, her Dean's Representative caught the two sentences, and without contacting the student or the student's major professor, she reported the student to the Dean of Students Office and charged her with plagiarism. The student and her major professor came to me, but the best advice I could give was that they HAD to find her guilty because technically speaking she WAS guilty. I have a habit of keeping ALL dissertation drafts of students on whose committee I serve until the student graduates. This is actually the first time this practice has saved a student from a terrible fate. The three of us (the student, her major professor and me) pulled out all of the previous drafts of the student's work, and we were able to piece together the series of events that had led to the two unwanted and undocumented sentences in the student's dissertation. We requested and were granted a meeting with the Dean of Students to explain the situation. After the explanation and the presentation of my documentation showing the evolution of the document and the exact point at which the accidently plagiarism occurred, the Dean of Students Office ruled that the student was "Guilty" (which I guess they HAD to do this) but with NO sanctions. This meant that she did not even have to wait to graduate.

There are several things about this incident that are very troubling to me:

1. Why did the Dean's Representative go to the Dean of Students Office without even a call to the student's major professor? I find this especially disturbing given that she was in the proposal meeting when the Wikipedia citation was discussed. I HAVE been in similar situations while serving on doctoral advisory committees both within and outside of our program. My standard action is to call the student's major professor and let them know that there are incidences of suspected plagiarism in the student's document, and that they MUST address this to avoid a charge of plagiarism against the student. I consider this warning a matter of professional courtesy. It is not as if this document were being submitted for publication at the point of a dissertation draft submitted to a committee.
2. It troubles me that this happened and COULD potentially happen to one of my students. Since that time, I require my students to use a plagiarism checker program prior to submitting their dissertation draft to the members of their doctoral advisory committee. My program of choice is Ithenticate. Thankfully, LSU in recent years has purchased a site license for this program. It is available to all faculty and with the recommendation of the major professor, any doctoral student at LSU can also use the

program free of charge. When (or sometime before) my doctoral students complete their general examination, I routinely get access for them to Ithenticate and insist that they use it BEFORE they submit anything to the members of their doctoral advisory committee.

3. I am also troubled that this young woman has a conviction for plagiarism on her academic record. If she ever decides to pursue a position in academia, this COULD be a major problem for her. I appreciate the way that the Dean of Students Office handled the situation. I would say that she received the best verdict that the system would allow them to give her. However, I am troubled that there was not a way to have her cleared of all charges given that the explanation was adequate to justify assignment of no sanctions.

LESSON NUMBER 10: PROTECT YOUR STUDENTS FROM PLAGIARISM—SOMETIMES THIS MEANS PROTECTING THEM FROM THEMSELVES

The best way I have found to do this is to insist (no REQUIRE) that they process their document through a plagiarism checker program before it goes to members of the doctoral advisory committee. What if your institution does not provide this access? Before LSU had the Ithenticate program available free to doctoral students, I required that ALL of my students purchase a subscription to Ithenticate and use it. They were (and are) required to submit the similarity report to me and explain how they have addressed each of the problems in the report. Once these have been addressed to my satisfaction, I insist that they run their document through the program again (with a considerably better outcome) and then I tell them to save a copy of this report in a safe place and keep it permanently. This way, if they are ever accused of plagiarism, they have the report to PROVE their due diligence in preparing their final dissertation.

CHAPTER 11

HARD HEADS

I went to school during the time when teachers and principals used corporal punishment as the standard method of punishment. My ninth grade Agriculture teacher had a saying that he liked to use whenever he caught students doing something that was inevitably going to lead to a paddling. He would say, "Hard heads make soft rear ends." It was still the age that if a teacher used any form of bad language in the classroom that was viewed as inappropriate, and it could easily lead to their dismissal. I am sure that a teacher today would most likely say, "Hard heads lead to sore asses," but not then. Well, paddling is rarely used in any school today (It still is not against the law, just against most school district policies.), and we certainly do not use punishment like this in doctoral study. After all, our students are all adults, and mostly successful professionals besides. That does not mean some of them are NOT hard-headed.

I served as a member of a doctoral advisory committee for a young woman who in the most extreme way met the characteristic of "Hand-headed." She had identified a data source for her proposed study that she wanted to use as her dissertation research, but the data source she had planned to use was one that I knew to be very unreliable. In fact, this was an organization with which I had been involved for the 15 years since I first arrived at LSU. The management of this organization depended heavily on faculty contracts to fund their operations, and they

Mentoring Doctoral Students in Higher Education:
An International Perspective, pages 43–46.
Copyright © 2025 *Michael F. Burnett*
Published under exclusive licence by Emerald Publishing Limited
ISBN: 979-8-88730-847-0 (PB); 979-8-88730-848-7 (HB); 979-8-88730-849-4 (EPDF)

were very long on promise and very short on delivery. When she first came to her committee to propose the use of this organization as her data source, I expressed very serious concerns both privately to the student's major professor and to the student and publicly in the proposal meeting. The student assured her major professor and the committee (including me) that she had "Seen" the data and that it met all the needed criteria for using it for her dissertation. I was NOT convinced, but I was not willing to refuse to approve the proposal.

A few weeks later, the student and her major professor came to me in a panic asking what they could do to solve a serious problem. It seems that when she received her data set, more of the data was "Missing" than was "Present." In other words, the data set was virtually worthless. I reminded her that she said she had seen the data set and that it was all there. She admitted that she took the word of a representative of the organization and that it was a mistake to do so. In other words, she lied to her committee. Her next question was "What do I do now?" Most of the data DID exist, but in a different data base owned by a different organization. As I saw the situation and conveyed to them (the student and her major professor) she could abandon the study and write another proposal OR her major professor could attempt to get access for her to the data base which housed a lot of the missing data. The only caveat was that she had to look up the variables separately for each member of her sample one at a time. "That will take hours!" she almost screamed. "Dozens of hours" was my response.

The good news is that she DID get her data, and she did get her degree. Also, I did spot check some of the data just to be sure that she did not simply fabricate the information. I am confident that she really did search for the data.

I worked with a man several years later that exhibited some of the same qualities but failed to get his data for a very different reason. This student was older than me, had worked as a highly successful professional for many years, and exuded self-confidence in his ability to complete his study. However, he had identified a study that would involve getting data from individuals working in the private sector. I cautioned him that organizations in the private sector are notoriously hesitant to participate in research activities. There are all kinds of concerns: industrial espionage, bad public relations, job turnover, etc. His response to my caution was that he had a personal contact in each of the organizations, and they had all assured him that getting access to their employees would be no problem—famous last words! He wrote a very good proposal and submitted it to his doctoral advisory committee. It was easily approved, and the moment of truth came soon afterward. He started making the rounds to the organizations that had "agreed" to allow him access to collect data from their employees. There were several of them and when the first couple said that their CEO had overruled their decision to allow him to study their employees, he was undaunted. We met, but he assured me that the others would let him into their organizations to do his research. To make a long story short—EVERY ONE OF THEM pulled out! Here he was with an excellent proposal and no data and no prospect of getting any data.

I want to be clear about this man. He did NOT complain, he did NOT whine, he did NOT even curse. He just rolled up his sleeves and went to work on a new proposal. The difference was that this time he had written authorization to use the employees (this time in the public sector) before he wrote the proposal. I do not believe that he doubted my expertise when he went forward with the first proposal. I simply believe that he trusted his contacts and their authority to grant him access to their respective companies. In fact, I think THEY believed they had the authority to grant him this access. He took responsibility for his mistake and wrote a new proposal without a minute of complaining. I consider this man to be a friend today, and I hope he feels the same way. I am sure that it is obvious he did receive his degree and he completed an excellent dissertation. Reality is that the organizations from whom the CEOs refused to participate failed to gain some information that could have been very useful to them.

Another young woman with whom I worked wrote and gained approval for her proposal, collected her data, and successfully analyzed the data to address the study objectives. However, when it came to writing the results of the study, she simply would not listen to my advice. One of my standard practices in helping a student get ready for the presentation of their dissertation research to their doctoral advisory committee is to meet with them regularly and think of as many questions as I can that MIGHT be asked in their final examination (the dissertation presentation). For example, I might ask the student, "If a member of the committee asked you this question regarding the results you have written, how would you respond?" I try to think of ANYTHING that might be raised by a member of the committee, and then we discuss how the student might respond. Many of these things are purely hypothetical, but with this student she treated each of these questions as a reason to add another one to three pages to the dissertation. For weeks, I tried to convince her that she did NOT need to add a response for every question I raised regarding her research, but to no avail. Finally, I just told her that I was not going to raise any more questions to help her prepare for the exam because each question led to an unnecessary expansion to the dissertation. She did pass the exam, but to date she has been unable to publish her work because she cannot get an article under 40 pages. It started at more than 63 pages, and I have managed to whittle it down to about 40. The journal she has targeted only allows 15 pages—Hard-headed!

LESSON NUMBER 11: IT IS OKAY FOR A STUDENT TO BE HARD-HEADED IF THEY ARE WILLING TO PAY THE PRICE

Some people say that hard-headedness and persistence are just two names for the same trait. I disagree. In my view, persistence is knowing the circumstances, accepting that the task will be difficult, and working tirelessly to achieve that task. To me hard-headedness has more of an element of willful disregard for the reality of circumstances (for example the reluctance of private sector organizations to participate in research). Please don't think that I mean to be harshly critical of hard-headed people, I have on occasion been one myself. However, like the man I discussed in the previous section, I have been willing to pay the price when my hard-headedness sent me down a wrong path. It is when a person does not want to pay the price, that I think it becomes a negative trait. For example, a PTA board at one of my children's schools wanted to do a certain project for a fundraiser, and we discussed it at one of our board meetings. The principal of the school (who I learned later as I got acquainted with him was a very good man) warned us that this project had been tried at this school multiple times and it had always failed terribly. As I saw it, we had essentially three options:

1. Abandon this project and find something else to use for fundraising (probably described as "Discretion—the better part of valor");
2. Investigate the project thoroughly and try to determine why it had failed previously at this school and then work to avoid making the same mistakes made earlier (probably described as persistence using my definition); or
3. Ignore the principal's warning and go forward with the project immediately (hard-headed based on the way I define it).

When you have a student who you think is being hard-headed, explain to them the difference between persistence and hard-headed and make sure you tell them that if they cannot deliver, they will have to pay the price.

CHAPTER 12

HANDICAPS

The Merriam-Webster online dictionary defines handicap as: "a disadvantage that makes achievement unusually difficult" (Merriam-Webster), and I suppose this is a fair definition when it comes to some of the circumstances that many doctoral students face during their programs. However, I believe that many more students deal with handicaps while they are enrolled in their doctoral programs than are ever diagnosed, identified, or acknowledged. I do not mean to suggest that we give less consideration for the things that are typically referred to as handicaps such as blindness, deafness, loss of limbs, etc. What I am suggesting is that we give much more consideration to other handicaps that occur/exist while a student is pursuing their doctorate.

I worked with a young man who was legally blind, and while he was registered with the Office of Disability Services (ODS) on campus (a group that does an excellent job of advocating for students on campus), he did not like to use the ODS to demand accommodations from his professors. This young man could see somewhat. However, when it came to reading, he required a very large font to enable him to read what was on a piece of paper. I first noticed him holding a paper I had distributed in class very close to his eyes attempting to read the information printed there. I waited until after class, and I asked him about what I had seen. It was then that he explained to me that he was registered with the ODS but that he tried not to demand accommodations. He said that he had a reader at home that raised the font large enough for him to read. I asked what size font he needed, and we eventually arrived at the point that I knew if I brought him a copy of all materials distributed in class enlarged to essentially fill an 11 by 17 page, he would be able to read the information. I asked my assistant to purchase a ream of 11 by 17 paper, and subsequently brought one copy to each class session printed on that paper. I did the same with tests, and I made sure that he was able to sit near the front of the classroom so that he could see the PowerPoint slides more easily. I also enlarged the font size on most of my PowerPoint slides, but I did not tell him this. I also made sure he knew that if he needed any other accommodations, he only had to let me know. This young man became one of my doctoral advisees, and he did complete his doctorate. His "handicap" certainly made his progress a little slower in some circumstances, but it seems to me that his handicap was better characterized as the faculty members who refused to provide him the needed accommodations without being forced to do so by the ODS. I have encountered a number of requested accommodations over the last 43 years, some requested by students, and some submitted through the ODS. I have only found one requested accommodation that I simply could not in good conscience accept. A student who had gained admission without approval of the program (something that is not supposed to happen) had then registered with the ODS on some basis of which I am unaware. She then requested that she be permitted to complete the program without attending class—at all! She wanted all instruction in all courses to be delivered to her individually. That was a time when some of our courses were online, but many were not. I was not willing to teach her the content of each of my courses on an individual basis, and I was unwilling to demand that my faculty members deliver their instruction to her in this manner.

We once had an undergraduate student in our teacher preparation program who simply refused to make a presentation in front of a class—any class. I met with the young man and asked him to consider how he would be a teacher if he could not speak in front of a group. After some exploration with which our faculty assisted him, he found another area with which he was comfortable. This is not particularly surprising since a Washington Post article identified that public speaking is the number one fear among U. S. citizens (Ingraham, C., January 7, 2010). In any case, he was not likely to be able to be a successful teacher without being able to speak to groups.

By the same token, I could not see how a person could successfully complete a doctoral program without being able to participate in group instruction. Even the online courses included group activities, and this is the part to which she had the objection. Without this accommodation she left the program.

If we use the definition of handicap from the beginning of this chapter, I have worked with a number of students who had significant handicaps although not officially classified as such by the ODS. One man with whom I worked filled two full time positions for the university for more than two years, had two back surgeries, lost his wife, and had significant damage to his house from one of the hurricanes that hit Baton Rouge. For a time while he was unable to come to work after one of his surgeries, I met with him at his home a couple of afternoons each week to work on his dissertation. He did finish his degree and did so with true excellence. In fact, I find his dissertation to be one of the finest that I have ever directed. Oh yes, for more than 10 years the Graduate School had his dissertation posted on their website as a model social science dissertation.

Another young man in our School was one of the most challenging students I have ever taught. I do not mean that in a negative light. He was brilliant to the point that he really challenged me in class. He was completely professional in doing this, but he thought in ways that were different; and he, consequently, found new ways to view the concepts taught in class. This is a quality that I value very highly among my students. He asked questions that made me take another look at the concepts and often view them differently. His assignments were always completed at an exceptionally high level of quality, but they were on occasions submitted late. In fact, as I learned later from his major professor, he had long-cycling bipolar disorder, and there were times when he was unable to leave his home. I know that he could have had this diagnosis submitted to the ODS and received some accommodations, but when I learned of his condition (handicap if you prefer) I made every effort to work with him to identify and meet his needs.

Each of these I have mentioned did or could qualify for officially approved accommodations. However, what about the student who had a teenage child that attempted suicide (she was unsuccessful, thankfully.)? This was definitely "a disadvantage that makes achievement unusually difficult" (Merriam-Webster). He and his wife were on suicide watch 24/7 for some time after the incident.

Also, what about the student who lost her home (down to the concrete slab) to a hurricane? This student was almost three years in recovering to the point that she was able to make substantial progress in her program again. Fortunately, she was able to get approval from the Graduate School for a time limit extension, and she did complete her Ph.D. with that time limit extension.

What about the student whose mother was diagnosed with terminal cancer, and she was the primary caregiver for her Mother for more than three years? When her Mother passed, she took a few months to grieve; and when she tried to come back to her doctoral program, she had exceeded her time limit. The Graduate School was only willing to give her a ONE semester extension, and she was unable to finish in that time frame. I would consider her situation to be a handicap based on the definition cited. I personally believe that the Graduate School made an insensitive and grievous error in the decision they made to deny this student at least a one-year time limit extension, and I did fight for the extension through four Graduate Deans, but without success. However, when I made the case to our current Graduate Dean, he saw the logic of the request and approved her readmission and an appropriate time limit extension. She starts this Fall.

What about the student who lost his first major professor to suicide and his second, third, and fourth major professors to the faculty members leaving LSU for other institutions? When we became acquainted through his enrollment in one of my courses, he was on his fifth major professor who promised to stay with him no matter what. However, as he was nearing the submission of his proposal to the members of his committee, again his major professor left LSU. By that point, I was serving as his Co-Chair, and the student and I continued the work on his proposal and subsequently his dissertation. We did have to find someone to serve as his Co-Chair since he was in a doctoral program in another college. We did find someone in that department who was willing to allow us to continue the study mostly unhampered. The student did finish his doctorate, and I later hired him as an adjunct faculty member in my department. He was an excellent teacher.

What about the man who lost his job as a result of downsizing in his organization? Unfortunately, this man (among others released from the organization) was at a stage in his career that made it difficult to find other employment. Losing his job was definitely a handicap. After a period of adjustment, this gentleman used his severance pay to pursue teacher certification as well as his doctorate. He was not one of my students although I was a member of his doctoral advisory committee. The last I heard from him he was a very successful and happy high school teacher.

What about the student who was very active and vocal in his support of the student rights movement in China in 1989? When the Tiananmen Square Massacre occurred (History.com Editors, June 9, 2020), he feared that when he returned to China after completing his doctorate, his life would be in jeopardy for his activist stance in support of the human rights movement. This certainly created a handicap for him in terms of making progress in his program. A couple of years later, he received notification through the Chinese government that his Father was dying, and he needed to come home if he wanted to see his Father before he died. He literally did not know if he would make it back when he left for China. He did make it back, and he finished his doctorate within a few years. However, he clearly preferred to stay in the United States after his degree was completed. One of his friends from graduate school heard from him recently, and he is a highly successful faculty member at a university in the United States.

LESSON NUMBER 12: RECOGNIZE CIRCUMSTANCES THAT CAUSE HANDICAPS AMONG STUDENTS AND ACCOMMODATE THEIR NEEDS WHENEVER YOU CAN

Many students face difficulties while they are enrolled in a doctoral program. To some extent, this is just life. However, if you see students facing situations that are "a disadvantage that makes achievement unusually difficult" (Merriam-Webster), do what you can to help and accommodate their needs in the difficulties. The help may be nothing more than being someone with whom the student can talk. However, the help you provide will pay big dividends to the student, to you, and to the program.

CHAPTER 13

THE GREEN-EYED MONSTER

Iago says to Othello in the famous play by Shakespeare, "O beware, my lord, of jealousy; It is the green-eyed monster which doth mock the meat it feeds on."

—*(Shakespeare, W. 1975/1622).*

We had a member of our faculty for a time while I was serving as the Director of the School who would have rivaled Iago as the most effective manipulator and liar in history (Okay, that is an overstatement). However, she seemed to be truly driven by jealousy, and she used a lot of lies and deceits to accomplish her goals. I have to admit that I was duped for a time, like many of the faculty in our unit. One of my colleagues and a close friend was the only faculty member in the unit who was not fooled by this person for even a moment. In fact, she tried to warn me, but she did it in such a subtle manner that I did not get the true meaning until most of the faculty members in the School were buried in the manure this faculty member had been shoveling. Her first priority seemed to be that ALL of the doctoral students in the School should be her advisees. She then wanted to keep the ones she deemed worthy and dispose of the rest.

Very early in her time at LSU she was assigned to team-teach a course with one of the School's most honorable faculty members (Let's call him Faculty A).

I should have known that something was wrong when she began dropping casual hints about his inconsistent and questionable behavior. This man was widely known for his exceptional honor and integrity, and I had personally known him for more than two decades with NO incidents that even came close to a breach of ethics on his part. I passed it off as just an inexperienced young faculty member.

Another of our faculty who was recognized as the best teacher in the program (Let's call her Faculty B) fell victim to rumors about her poor teaching effectiveness. Our "Green-Eyed" faculty member on one occasion shared with me things that students had told her about Faculty B, but she would not tell me which students. It seemed that she made deliberate efforts to discredit every faculty member in the School on some basis. At some point in her first few years here at LSU she was in my office complaining about or spreading rumors about every member of the faculty. Faculty C and I had a history of disagreements, sometimes rather extreme, and she openly criticized him to me, probably to get on my good side since I was the unit administrator.

I learned sometime later that she had also been criticizing me as well as creating and spreading rumors about me. It seems that she viciously criticized my handling of virtually everything in the School. However, the most baseless and vicious rumor she spread about me was that I was sleeping with my students. This was not true, but she used this as well as other criticisms in efforts to convince my students to change from me to her as their major professor. I think she saw my greatest strength was in the area of graduate advising, so this is where she attacked me most.

Several of my students came to me and told me that she had tried to convince them to change to her as their advisor. She used a variety of arguments ranging from my being too busy to serve as their advisor to my obvious lack of honor since I was sleeping with my students. My response when any of these students came to me to discuss changing to her was the same that it always was when a student was considering changing major professors—if you feel this is what is best for your degree completion you have my blessing. If you want me to stay on the committee I will, but if you want me to step away completely that is fine also. There were no hard feelings toward the student. Some of them did change to her as their advisor. Unfortunately, when she had them, if she decided that they were more trouble than they were worth, she advised them to take actions that would jeopardize their program. One student was advised to take a course for which he did not have the background. He failed the course, and I couldn't help but feel she did this to him intentionally since she had decided he would need more help getting through the program than she was willing to give. Many of my students came to me and told me what she said and how she tried to convince them to change to her as their major professor. Most of my students simply told her no, but some said yes, and more than one of them paid a similar price as the one cited earlier.

My students were not the only ones she tried to take, but I had more so more of them were mine. Additionally, the students who changed to her from another major professor were not the only ones she sabotaged. Any student that she perceived as weak was in jeopardy. She made deliberate efforts to separate me from her advisees completely, especially my former students, by trying to convince them to remove me from the committee. One student who I had helped a great deal with her proposal development while she was enrolled in my courses came to me very upset. She sat in my office and told me through tears that her major professor had told her that she had to remove me from the committee. She said she was simply given no choice.

I personally believe that her primary motivation in all these actions was based in jealousy. I think she envied Faculty A for his stellar reputation, Faculty B for her teaching excellence, and me for my reputation as a graduate advisor. With us and the other faculty members in the School, the thing she seemed to attack was their greatest area of strength.

If a person did not have a particular area of strength, they seemed to be used as pawns to set up other faculty. For example, when she had an offer from another university, she came to me and informed me that she had an offer and that if I would give her a $15,000.00 raise, she would agree to stay. I did talk with the Dean about her ultimatum, and his question was whether or not that was where I wanted to spend my money. When I told him that I did not have the money in my budget, he said that I had my answer for her in that case. When I informed her about my feedback from the Dean, she was not happy. At that point I just told her that she had to do what she thought was the right thing for her, but there would be no pay raise. Apparently, she convinced another faculty member who had the years to be eligible for retirement to retire immediately. The two of them left within 24 hours of one another—her as a resignation and him as a retirement—but he made his retirement effective one day prior to the effective date of her resignation. He even informed me that he chose the effective date to do as much damage to the School as possible. However, the School was stronger for the loss of both of these people, even if there were some short-term difficulties.

LESSON NUMBER 13: WHEN YOU ENCOUNTER PEOPLE WHO PLAY DIRTY, DON'T PLAY. YOU CAN'T WIN, BECAUSE EVEN IF YOU WIN YOU LOSE

I wish I had realized much earlier what this faculty member was doing. Much pain and discomfort might have been avoided for me and several of my colleagues as well as the students caught in the middle of these situations. People throughout all organizations have faced similar situations dealing with this type of individual. In his book, <u>The No Asshole Rule</u>, Robert Sutton makes the point that there are assholes in virtually every workplace, and he emphasizes that we should either remove them from the organization or take steps to ensure that they are reformed to a less destructive character. He distinguishes between a person who occasionally does things that might label them as an Asshole and those that behave this way virtually all the time. He calls these people who behave like Assholes occasionally "Temporary Assholes" and emphatically makes the point that everyone does things, once in a while, that might give them this label. However, he says that a "Certified Asshole" is a person who has, "a history of episodes that end with one 'target' after another feeling belittled, put down, humiliated, disrespected, oppressed, deenergized, and generally worse about themselves." (Sutton, 2007, p. 11). Sutton further says that, ." . . if someone consistently takes actions that leave a trail of victims in their wake, they deserve to be branded as certified assholes" (Sutton, 2007, p. 11–12). If anyone ever deserved the label of "Certified Asshole," I would say that she did.

The world is replete with sayings about dealing with this type of person. Richard Branson, a prominent business magnate and author, says, "Play fair, be prepared for others to play dirty, and don't let them drag you into the mud" (AZ Quotes). Former U.S. presidential candidate Adlai Stevenson made the comment "He who slings mud generally loses ground" (Goodreads, January 12, 2021). A well-known Christian author and speaker, Ravi Zachasias, carried this a little further when he said, "When You Sling Mud at another person, you not only get your hands dirty, you also lose ground." (Focusfied)

In his book, Nasty People: How to Stop Being Hurt by Them without Becoming One of Them" Jay Carter very aptly makes the point that you should never try to play their game because they are better at it than you, and they will always win (Carter, 1989); and my experience has confirmed this to me. Literally, this week I was in a committee meeting, and my opinion was clearly the opposite of the majority of the group. I made every effort to address the issues raised, many of which I felt were invalid, but I did not allow my arguments to become personal attacks on the other members of the committee. I simply tried to explain why I was taking the position I expressed. As the meeting progressed it deteriorated into a personal assault on me. I was told by a person who had very little experience in the methodology proposed that she knew that subjects would not respond. She did not express concern about the number and validity of responses. She insisted that she knew for an absolute fact that subjects would not respond and those who did would not respond honestly. I do not see how she knew this, and the one committee member who should have known better apparently did not know better. Specifically, two members of the committee completely discounted my experiences and expertise by claiming to know more about the methodology than I did. Oh well—at no point in the discussion did I question these individuals' knowledge or expertise, but they did exactly this to me. I was insulted, and I had to quickly make a decision as to how I would react to this treatment. I could simply hush and let it pass or I could let them know the inappropriateness of their comments, at least in my opinion. I told this individual that I thought the reason we were having a committee meeting was to hear all sides of the issue. I reminded her that at no time had I been disagreeable or personally insulting to those with differing views while expressing my views. I then told the group that they knew my position and that I would hush, which I did. I could have retaliated, but then I would have been playing their game. I would have lost even if I had made greater attacks, because my hands would have been dirty, and the group would still have voted against my position. So, it would have been a double loss. The student was not approved by the committee to do the proposed study, and rather than compromise the integrity of her study she changed to another topic.

CHAPTER 14

SOMETIMES YOU CAN TRUST THE COVER

An old phrase advises that, "You Can't Judge a Book by Its Cover." Generally, this is given as advice or sometimes as a warning that just because a book has an attractive cover does not necessarily mean that what is inside will be a good read. It can also mean that you cannot judge the character and worth of a person by what you see on the surface (Ky Phrase). Sometimes, a student can seem on the surface to be someone who will literally set the world afire in terms of the impact they will have on the profession, but time will show that this view was an illusion. It could be that they encountered a traumatic situation in their personal life that changed the trajectory of their life, so please do not read this as an indictment of students who do not achieve at their expected levels. Frankly, I think that based on my master's advisor's recommendation, I was probably a disappointment to many of my doctoral professors. I think they may have expected me to pursue national professional leadership positions, and I might have done so if my circumstances had not changed so dramatically here at LSU.

There are, however, times when what you see is exactly what is there. A woman entered our undergraduate program after having worked in business for about 20 years. She brought with her one semester of credit from one of the smaller universities in Louisiana. In a period of five and one-half years, she completed a baccalaureate degree, a master's degree, and a Ph.D. degree in our program. She did this while maintaining a very high GPA. When she entered the doctoral program, she was told that she would be required to work with me as her major professor. She explained to the administrator who issued this mandate that he would not tell her who she had to work with because he did not do that with any other students. She said that if she was going to be treated differently, she would just go somewhere else. I was ambivalent about the issue. I would have been glad to work with her, but I was not lobbying for more students. In fact, she did not even select me as one of her committee members even though I taught her in four courses and eventually helped her with several of her data analysis issues.

What she appeared to be was a truly exceptional student and a person with very high potential as a faculty member in higher education. She was also rather independent. She was place bound to the Baton Rouge area by her family situation, so when she completed her doctorate, she accepted a position in one of the local vocational technical schools. After a couple of years, the man who was our unit head at the time (not the same one as when she entered) convinced the administration of the university to take a chance on her and allow us to hire her in a tenure-track faculty position even though her terminal degree was from LSU. It was one of the best decisions we ever made. Oh, and by the way, she is African American. She and I became very good friends and continue to be friends even though she has been retired for several years (about 10). I can say without equivocation that she is the best teacher we have ever had in our program, at least in the 43 years I have been here. During the time she was a member of our faculty, she was the only person of color on the faculty, but her presence did more to enhance our minority recruitment than anything else imaginable. If you really want to get serious about minority recruitment, hire some highly capable faculty of color. It sends all the right messages to students who were considering the program for pursuing their degree. Oh, and it does not just enhance minority recruitment. It sends the message to all student that you value diversity. Remember there are many different types of diversity. Perhaps they are Hispanic or gay or Asian or transgender, or etc. the message you are sending is that you not only accept diversity but also value it. The enrollment in our doctoral program during this time period reached 81 students (just doctoral) and was the fifth largest at LSU. Not bad for a program with only 10 faculty members.

LESSON NUMBER 14: DO NOT JUST ACCEPT DIVERSITY AMONG YOUR STUDENTS, STRIVE FOR IT—IT WILL GREATLY ENHANCE THE EDUCATION IN YOUR PROGRAM INCLUDING YOUR OWN LEARNING

I know that the person who appears to be great on the surface often ends in disappointment, and departments often regret having hired them or admitted them to the program. Think of the Heisman Trophy curse. The Heisman Trophy is awarded to the college football player that is judged to be the best in the country. The Heisman curse says that if a player wins the Heisman, their team will subsequently lose in their post-season game. However, it extends to the winner's career in the National Football League (Zavaleta, 2010).

This certainly does not mean that we should avoid those individuals (students or faculty) that seem to epitomize all the best qualities for which we are searching to improve the chances of success. Sometimes you **Can** judge a book by its cover, and what you see really is what you get.

CHAPTER 15

ABILITY IS NOT ENOUGH

Over the years I have seen a lot of reasons why students do complete their doctorate, but another very important issue is why students who are enrolled in doctoral programs do not finish their degrees. Sometimes we look at applicants who obviously have a high degree of achievement as well as innate ability, and we assume that this person will easily move through the program with little or no difficulties. However, in some cases we find that this exceptional student does not successfully complete the program. Over the years, I have seen quite a few students with high levels of ability that experienced significant problems in completing an educational program. The reasons behind their lack of success are almost as varied as those explaining lack of success among any other group of students. The one reason that should not be the cause of a doctoral student's lack of success is their capability.

I have actually known a few students who were admitted to our doctoral program who did not possess the capability to be successful, but there have been very few of these. One of these was a young man who was very pleasant but either did not prepare for his general examination or truly did not have the capability of learning the content. I teach a series of research methods, design, and data analysis courses that are required of all doctoral students in our program. Additionally, if I serve as a member of a student's doctoral advisory committee, my process for conducting my portion of the written exam is that I tell the student seven specific areas that they should study to be prepared for my written exam. From those seven areas, I choose five questions that are included on my portion of the written examination. The student can then choose three of the five questions to answer in an in-house testing environment without the use of resources. This young man did so poorly on the written exam that I could not agree to allow him to move forward to the oral portion of the exam. My area of the test was not the only one on which he performed poorly, so the committee agreed to let him re-do the written exam. This time I gave him the specific questions that he would need to answer for me. In fact, two of the three for which he needed to prepare were two of the ones he had answered (albeit poorly) on his first written exam. I also met with the student to let him know his errors from the first exam and to answer any questions he had for clarification. His next written exam was very little better than his previous exam. We did permit him to move to the oral portion of the exam this time, and he virtually answered nothing correctly in the oral. The committee simply had no choice but to report to the Graduate School that he had failed the exam. Understand that we want our students to be successful but not at the expense of quality performance. He was advised that continuing to another attempt to pass the general exam was likely to be unsuccessful. I know that many times when a doctoral student performs poorly on an exam, the reason can be traced to the preparation they were given by their major professor. However, in this case I worked directly with the student to be sure that he was prepared to perform well on my portion of the written exam. It was as if I had given him no guidance at all. I believe at that time the student was unable to perform at a satisfactory level on the general exam. I realize that there could have been some organic reason for his poor performance, but we could find no evidence of this situation. In defense of the program's admission procedure, this was a student who was admitted during a time that the Graduate School dramatically lowered their admission requirements, and our School had always (up until then) used the Graduate School requirements as our admission requirements. This was not the only student admitted during that time period, but soon afterwards, our School adopted our own admission criteria which exceeded the Graduate School minimums.

Essentially, the same thing happened with a young woman who was admitted during this period also. She was just by all appearances and evidence unable to successfully complete the general examination. These are by no means the only students who have failed the general examination in our program. However, these and a very few others are the only ones who simply seemed incapable of passing the general examination. Usually, an unsatisfactory performance can be traced to a situational issue. For example, I served on a doctoral committee for a man who just performed very poorly, but we learned that he was taking his examination during the time that his Brother, with whom he had a very close relationship, was dying of cancer. After his Brother passed away and a reasonable grieving period, he came back and re-tested on his general examination.

Students of very high ability are often perceived by their professors, including their doctoral advisors, as needing little or no guidance. It is true that they usually need less direct assistance with certain areas such as use of data analysis programs and just basic writing skills. However, in most aspects of degree program completion, these individuals are subject to very much the same difficulties and problems as any other students, and some that are unique to them. Some of these include:

1. The need for direction—Just because a person has a high level of ability does not automatically mean that they know the things that need to be done to complete a doctorate. Once they have a clear understanding of the path to reach their goal, they can usually move with deliberateness to finish the degree. One young man with whom I worked a few years ago was clearly giving me much more credit than I deserved for his progress in the program. I explained to him that he deserved the credit for completing the work—that I was just the "cartographer, and that my role and goal was simply to be sure that he had accurate maps showing the route to reach his destination. He was from another country, and he was not familiar with the term "cartographer." He became enamored with the term, and even included it in the very kind and generous acknowledgement he wrote to me when he finished his degree.

Another young man with whom I worked was extremely bright, and when my career path took me to another college and ultimately a different department on campus, he was encouraged to change from me as his major professor to another faculty member in my former program. I guess that his new major professor assumed that since he was a very bright and highly capable student, he needed little or no direction to be successful in the doctoral program. Nothing could have been further from the truth. Without regular meetings and direction in those meetings, he quickly settled into a condition of stasis. He was what I referred to earlier as on "Top Dead Center." As his time limit was running out, he came to me and said that his major professor would not meet with him to help him prepare a petition for a time limit extension. Without this extension he would be dropped from the Graduate School. I told him that I would help him prepare his petition, and we scheduled a meeting for that purpose. When he came to the meeting, he asked me if I would consider resuming my role as his major professor. I indicated that I would be happy to serve as his advisor, and we scheduled a regular meeting time to begin work on his dissertation. He had already completed his general examination, and he had actually completed much of the work on his dissertation. We received approval on the time limit extension, and within two semesters, he scheduled his final examination and successfully presented his dissertation to his graduate advisory committee. All he really needed was some regular direction and guidance. Not getting the study completed had nothing to do with his ability. It was simply the need for direction, and when he received this help, he moved forward with stunning speed. I honestly believe that without the help, he would have just left LSU without the degree. When I was a high school teacher, one of the topics I taught in some of my classes was basic welding skills. I first taught them how to weld in the classroom. Following this, we went to the lab, and they had to apply what they had learned in class. However, I carefully supervised them in lab and gave them instructions as they attempted to demonstrate their basic welding skills. This doctoral candidate knew (intellectually) how to do a dissertation. I know, I taught it to him in my courses. However, applying that knowledge to the actual conduct of a research study and preparation of this study into a dissertation did not come naturally after learning the academic information. It took some coaching and correction as he began practicing the skills. With the coaching, he produced an excellent study and received his degree.

2. The need for encouragement—Virtually every student enrolled in a doctoral program needs direction. They need that "Cartographer," because completing a Ph.D. is something they have never done before. As I have discussed earlier, the fact that you have never advised a doctoral student to completion is the reason that you need an experienced Co-Chair or a mentor when you complete your first doctoral advisee. In my 43 years as a doctoral advisor, I have only had the opportunity to work with a student who was completing a second doctorate once. These individuals do exist, and you may once in a long while have this opportunity, but this person (one completing a second doctorate) is very rare. The one with whom I worked needed very little direction from me. Oh, she did have to make the changes and adjustments to my preferences and research requirements, but she had been through the process and, being an excellent student, she made the adjustments quickly and easily.

Most doctoral students enter the program with a clear goal in mind. However, sometimes a person needs more than just a map showing the path leading to the completion of the degree. Sometimes they need one or more forms of encouragement. This may be encouragement that they CAN complete the degree. Alternatively, it may be encouragement that they still WANT to complete the degree. It may be a reminder of why they began the degree in the first place. As I have mentioned in this book previously, one of my professors at Ohio State was wont to remind us that completing a Ph.D. is 99% perspiration and only 1% inspiration. Accordingly, completing a doctorate can be a long and arduous journey. I know personally that 99% perspiration truly was a lot of hard work and translated into a difficult and rewarding journey (at least for me). Over the years, I have seen numerous incidents in which students succumbed to that hard work before they completed the degree.

I served as a member of the doctoral advisory committee for a young man who literally successfully completed his final examination (the presentation of the dissertation he had completed to his doctoral advisory committee). However, he had considerable editorial revisions to make in the document. After eight years of enrollment in the program when he was told he had passed the final examination and all that remained was some editorial "clean up" in his document, he loudly and rudely informed the committee that he would not make one more change in the document. He then walked out and walked away. Would encouragement have made a difference in his decision? Maybe or maybe not. I found it very hard to believe that he made the decision to walk away. He was not my advisee, and I believe that his advisor was a good person, but she was inexperienced in graduate advising.

I served as the doctoral advisor for a woman who lost literally everything she owned when her home flooded. This even included all the work she had completed on her dissertation proposal. She learned that her flood insurance covered only the structure—nothing on the contents of the house. In addition, her husband lost his job, and consequently she was the only source of income. She and her husband used the insurance money they received from the coverage on the structure to buy materials and they did the labor themselves. They then used the money they saved by doing the labor themselves to replace as much of the contents as they could. To say that she needed encouragement to remain in the program would be overstating the obvious. She requested and was granted a stop to the time limit clock while she recovered from the flood damage, but when time came for her to resume her program, I tried to provide her with as much encouragement as possible. This involved changing her dissertation research topic from one that would have been difficult to complete in her available time and with her available resources to one that was more practical under the circumstances. One of the key factors in providing the encouragement she needed to continue was helping her find a topic that was both doable and for which she could develop a passion to complete. She was a student that truly needed this passion for the research to maintain her motivation to complete the study. In her case she did find the topic and she did get the study finished in her available time to the satisfaction of both me and the members of her doctoral advisory committee.

Another young woman with whom I had the opportunity to work encountered a series of changes in her life that made her question whether or not the degree was still of high enough priority for her to continue. Chief among these changes was the birth of her first child. While it was not my place to say that she should place less importance on her family, it seemed to me that what she had done was lose sight of why she started the degree in the first place. When we met and she told me she was considering resigning from the program, I simply encouraged her to think carefully about why she first wanted to pursue the degree. I asked her to promise me that she would not take definitive action on her resignation until we had discussed the issue thoroughly. I gave her a few questions that I wanted her to consider at our next appointment. These included:

    a.   Why did you enroll in the program initially?
    b.   Five years from now when it is too late to resume the program, will you regret having left without the degree?

c. Are there realistic circumstances that could occur which would cause you to NEED this degree?
d. Will you have problems telling your children about leaving the program when they are old enough to ask about it? Will you wish you had completed the program as a role model for your children if for no other reason?

There are probably other issues that we discussed, but I know we discussed these at least. In the end, she decided to stay in the program, and she did exceptionally well. In fact, she won awards for her dissertation research.

Another woman with whom I worked was highly capable but had her self-confidence shaken by a faculty member who seemed to be intimidated by her ability. Unfortunately, she took his ill-intentioned criticism to heart and for a considerable time, I was not sure she would ever be able to move forward in the program. I seriously feared that she would resign from the program. She apparently believed that I was not unbiased regarding her performance and ability, therefore, no matter what I tried to repair her injured self-confidence, it did not work. Ultimately, I simply had to push her to move to the next step in the program. Happily, with no prompting on my part, the encouragement she needed came from one of her committee members. Once her self-confidence was restored, she moved deliberately to finish her degree with excellence.

I had the pleasure of working with a young man several years ago who was extremely bright but had a serious self-esteem issue. This student did not need encouragement at a few critical points along the path, he needed encouragement throughout the process. It may seem to you that this is a student who should have been left to "sink or swim." After all, you are not a babysitter, are you? When I say that he needed encouragement throughout the process, I am not suggesting that he needed an appreciably larger amount of time investment. What I do mean is simply that he had to be handled with a gentler approach.

Another student with whom I had the privilege of working was actually a master's student from another program. I do not know why she enrolled in my introductory research course, but by the end of the course I had become so impressed by her abilities that I WANTED to be a member of her graduate advisory committee. The final exams in all of my research courses are designed to be more akin to a standardized test than a course exam. There are a lot of questions (typically 60 to 75), and they are all designed as multiple-choice items. In my 43 years at LSU, I have taught this course more than 50 times, and there have only been five students who have made a perfect score on the test, and she is one of these five. Here is the problem, her major professor was directing her very first thesis, and she had engaged one of her friends that "knows everything." Unfortunately, he had never directed a student thesis to completion. All the students with whom he had worked had left without completing their degree and they all cited his harsh, critical, and overly demanding attitude as their reason for leaving the program without the degree. I watched her flounder for several months, and finally, in one of our counselling sessions (which had become fairly frequent by this point), I made some management decisions. Her major professor works just a few offices down the hall from me, and we are also friends, although not as close as she is with this young man who thinks he knows everything. Her committee (driven by the man who knows all) had expanded her study to the point that it was the equivalent of at least two dissertations. Here is what I did:

1. We established a regular meeting schedule,
2. I told her to bring both her purpose statement and objectives to our meeting as well as her measuring instrument,
3. She had a large number of concepts and items to investigate that had nothing to do with her purpose statement and objections,
4. We rewrote her purpose and objectives to clearly reflect the original goals and objectives of her study,
5. We went through her instrument and removed every item that did not contribute directly to her purpose and objectives,
6. I pressed the issue with her committee and reminded them that "this is a master's thesis—NOT a doctoral dissertation,"
7. The committee accepted that changes—in my opinion because the man on her committee had never had anyone in academics to stand up to him directly,
8. Like any bully, he backed off when directly confronted,
9. Once she had her proposal approved, I worked with her as her mento to get her through the completion and defense of her study.

Here is the real shame that resulted from this set of circumstances: she says that she will never pursue a doctorate because of the way she was treated in that other program. I have tried to convince her to come work with me, but she just says that she is burned out. I have heard from other faculty in his department that he is really not a "bad guy" and that it is "just his way" to be aggressive toward his students. This is what Sutton (2007) would call one of the most frequently cited excuses for the behavior of "certified assholes" (That is just how ____ is). say They say his bark is worse than his bite. However, I have seen many cases in which a really aggressive bark often causes the person to leave without even knocking on the door. That may be really good in preventing burglars from breaking into your home, but I do not feel that it is good if it scares a great student away from your program. By the way, I have told her that no matter what the paperwork says, she IS one of MY students. She seemed pleased with that.

In recent months (before she finished her thesis) she has landed a role on a popular television series. I told her that if I helped her finish this thesis, it would cost her "Big time." She asked what a little tenuously, and I replied that I wanted an autographed photo of her on the set in payment for helping her. After her thesis defense (which was highly successful), she brought me my photo. In fact, she paid double. I now have two great autographed photos displayed in my office. Ironically, the very next student that entered our doctoral program (when I just casually mentioned her name) said with incredulity, "Do you mean that you know _____." I replied, "Yes, I knew her before she was a star." Great story, isn't it? The fact is that every word of it is true. I got the star to review it just to be sure that I had it all accurate.

We have become very good friends, and seeing her experiences with me, her boyfriend recently transferred to our program, and he is now a student worker in our departmental office. I still remind her occasionally that I will be here when she is ready to do her doctorate. I hope I am anyway.

I had a student who was a member of the United States Marines. He was not on active duty, but as all marines that I have known tell me, "Once a Marine, always a Marine." There is no such thing as a former Marine. He was capable, knowledgeable, hard-working, and very self-assured. We had a great working relationship, and often if he did not get the work completed that he was assigned, I would tell him that if he came back without his completed work again, I would throw him out the window. We both knew I was kidding, especially since I could not have thrown him three feet if my life had depended on it. Another young man I advised was an aspiring Olympian (I have talked about him earlier), and after I had earned his trust, I would tell him that if he did not get his work done in a timely manner, I would take him to the track and let everyone see him outrun by an old man. That was even a bigger joke than throwing the Marine out of a window. I could not have outrun him in a 1500-meter race if I had a bicycle and a 1000-meter head start. I had to be careful about saying things like that until a close mentoring relationship had been established. The trust must be there, and it must run both ways. Saying things like this without the trust could cause serious damage to the confidence in his ability to complete the degree. It is all part of "knowing your students."

This young man was an American citizen, but many of the students with whom I have worked have been from a wide variety of other countries. You should always be careful to establish a close mentoring relationship with students from other countries before you begin making casual comments. In many of these countries (especially African countries in my experience) a faculty member's word is law. I have learned from numerous international students who have completed my courses that the reason they are so hesitant to disagree with me in class discussions is that they have been taught it is disrespectful to disagree with a person in a supervisory position over them and, that this is especially true regarding university faculty who are held in the highest esteem in their home country. My advice would be to tread lightly with casual comments until the relationship is established.

3. Personal health problems—As is true in accomplishing any goal in life, sometimes personal health problems become an obstacle. You can well

imagine that in more than 40 years as a doctoral advisor, I have seen numerous different personal health issues. Many of these have been mentioned in other lessons described in this book, but for sake of the current lesson's clarity I will mention some of them again.

One man with whom I worked went through a severe back injury that resulted in multiple surgeries to help ameliorate his back pain to the point that he was physically able to complete his dissertation and his degree. He was successful in this endeavor, and if you look up the definition of perseverance in the dictionary, you might find his picture there (just kidding). I can say without hesitation that I have never known anyone with more determination to complete the degree and more focus on the quality of the work that he completed. His study remains as one of the best with which I have been associated. The funny thing is that very shortly after he finished his degree, he retired.

Not every case of illness works out as well as the previous example. One gentleman in our program (not one of my advisees although I was on the committee) went into full renal failure while pursuing his degree. The good news is that he did receive a successful kidney transplant. However, he never returned to the program after his surgery.

Another young woman (again, not one of my advisees, but I was a member of her committee) had a significant health issue, the specifics about which I was and still am unaware. This health issue caused an interruption in her program near the end of her time limit. The health problem was of enough length that her time limit and her one-year extension both expired, and she walked away from the program. If the health issue was of enough severity, she could have requested and possibly received a second time limit extension. I wish she had requested this second extension, and I cannot tell you why she did not. I do not know if she was unaware of the possibility of a second extension or if she just was not physically up to pursuing the degree any further.

We welcomed an exceptional young woman into the program, but she learned very early in her academic progress that she had a relatively rare form of cancer. Most of the doctors in this area gave her no hope for survival. However, she sought experimental and extreme treatment possibilities. She found one and pursued it with an unbelievable degree of optimism and vigor. When she returned to Baton Rouge, she called and scheduled a meeting with me to discuss returning to the program. However, when she went back for her three-month check, the cancer had metastasized to several other organs. She survived for about six months. Actually, a very similar situation occurred with another of our students. She was treated locally, and she did not leave the program or her employment. She literally worked to within three days of her death. She was my daughter's 4-H agent, and the children all adored her. The weekend before she passed, she accompanied a group of sixth graders (including my daughter) to a weekend camp. Sunday evening when I picked up my daughter at the Parish 4-H office was the last time I ever saw her. I guess you could not say that these students chose to leave the program, but they also did not finish the program.

We have had other students in our program who had varying degrees of mental health issues. Probably the most frequent mental health issues I have seen among our students are clinical depression and bipolar disorder. One of our students was a graduate assistant and during a manic state he caused an incident that resulted in him being terminated from his assistantship. Later that year, he was in an altercation with police officers (again while in a manic state) that led to him being wounded. He survived, but he left the doctoral program. I know, you probably would say that he should have left, and maybe so. However, the point here is that people leave the program for many different reasons, and a mental health condition is one of them.

4. Family health problems—Another situation that often causes students to leave the program is that of family health issues. One of my doctoral advisees learned during the dissertation phase of his program that his wife required a liver transplant for her survival. He did what he could academically but being available for her care at any moment as well as the stress associated with potentially facing the loss of his spouse of more than 30 years was a dramatic interference to his academic progress. Over a period of two years, she finally made it to the top of the transplant list only to pass away before a matching liver became available. After an appropriate period of grieving, he returned to the program, and he did complete his degree. As he said to me on multiple occasions, he would have gladly traded the doctorate to have her back, but that was not within his control.

Another young man was enrolled in the program and was faced with the situation of his teenage daughter attempting suicide. I have mentioned him before; but suffice it to say that his daughter's mental health condition was his reason for leaving the program, and he never returned to his degree program.

Recently, a young woman was enrolled in our program when she learned that her mother was terminally ill. For more than three years she was her mother's primary caregiver. After her mother passed away, she tried to return to the program, but her time limit had expired and even one semester past this. We petitioned the Dean of the Graduate School to allow her some additional time to finish the program. However, he was only willing to approve one semester which, with the semester already past, was the equivalent of a one-year extension of time. One semester was just not enough time to finish her degree and though I talked until I was "Blue in the Face," the Dean would not budge. Consequently, she walked away. I would like to specifically point out the name of the Dean who was so totally uncaring regarding this student's adversity, but then that would be unethical, and I certainly do not want to emulate him. LSU recently hired a new Graduate School Dean, and I renewed and strengthened my petition for this woman, and she will now have the opportunity to resume her program this Fall. See—persistence does pay off—at least sometimes.

5. Change of focus/reason for the degree—A young man whom I was advising seemed to be moving painfully slowly after he transferred from my previous program to my current program specifically for the purpose of working with me. We met weekly for about three months and seemed to be no further on the dissertation proposal than when we started until finally, he came to his appointment one week and told me that he was resigning from the program. When I asked why he explained to me that he simply did not have the passion for the degree that he had earlier. I went through the same process as with the student I described earlier. When he came back for the follow-up meeting to let me know his feelings after thinking about the issues, I asked him to consider, he said that he just did not see how the degree would benefit him. He said that he and his partner were planning to retire as soon as they were eligible under the requirements of their respective organizations. After they retire, they plan to move abroad where they have already purchased property. We parted company on friendly terms, and I sincerely wished him the best in his future. Not everyone plans to remain in the workforce into their seventies, and I respect his decision. I told him this and asked him to stay in contact to let me know how things were going for him. I also told him that IF he changed his mind, to please let me know as soon as possible. You may wonder why I use this specific example. Well, no matter how capable the student is and no matter how much you try to encourage them, sometimes they just decide to leave the program without the degree. If they seem to have a clear minded decision, just let it go.

6. Pressure of higher expectation—From my earliest memories of school, I have always been a very good student. I do not know if I was good at being a student because I enjoyed it or if I enjoyed being a student because I was good at it. In any case, I have always been a good student. This was true in elementary school, in junior high school, in high school (I graduated seventh in a class of 306 students), in my baccalaureate program, in my master's program, and then came the doctoral program. I am not suggesting that I had insurmountable difficulties in my doctoral program but pursuing a degree that is only held by about 1.2% of the adult population in the United States is enough to shake the confidence of most people. In fact, during my first full term at Ohio State one of my professors asked me to meet with him in his office. The topic that he wanted to discuss with me was my previous academic difficulties. I was under a great deal of pressure to prove myself before that, but after that meeting, the pressure was increased many-fold. It would have been very easy at that point to simply resign, pack my bags, and head back for South Carolina and

a high school teaching job. Thankfully that same term I had a professor who returned the first paper I had written for him and noted on that paper that he offered very few comments since I already write as well as or better than he does. I was not seriously considering leaving the program because of one negative experience with a faculty member, but the comments from the other faculty member about my writing certainly helped to keep that thought out of my mind.

I have remembered that experience, and I always try to find something good to say to all students, including the highly capable students who you might think do not need reinforcement. I try to do this especially for those students who are very early in the program. This may be on a paper or even just verbally. I DO hold extremely high expectations for my doctoral advisees, but I do not hit them with this as they walk through the door. As I may have mentioned previously, I have heard from students in the past that they know that I am very demanding, but they know that I make these demands before they go TO an exam so that we maximize their likelihood of success ON the exam.

I have found that highly capable students are often more susceptible to this problem than the lesser capable doctoral students. (Yes, I know that all doctoral students are highly capable, but I am talking about this from a relative standpoint.) These students have been accustomed to being at or near the top of every academic activity of which they have been a part. Now, all of a sudden, they are no longer the brightest in the room. I have seen undergraduate students who were valedictorians or salutatorians of their high school class be completely devastated by achieving only a 3.3 GPA in their first semester of college. This very situation happened to one of these students from my high school graduating class. The same kind of thing happens with doctoral students. I could name off the top of my head at least a half-dozen students who walked away because they were disappointed in their initial performance in the program. I am not talking about those who were dropped from the Graduate School due to unsatisfactory performance. These are students who simply did not perform up to their own expectations based on their previous performances.

7. Too many options—One of the things that I have often heard and even said about very bright children is that they can do anything they want to do. It is a wonderful thing when a person has the capability to literally do anything they want to do. They can be a surgeon, a lawyer, a psychiatrist, a business manager, an engineer, a college professor, etc. If you are one of these people you are probably saying right now that it is both a blessing and a curse. During the time that I was in my doctoral program, one of my friends from another program who was graduating applied for a faculty position and learned that the program had more than 600 applicants for that one position. How in the world do you sort through that many applicants? In my experiences, about one-fourth of the applicants

for any position are simply unqualified for the position. I served on the search committee in the mis-1980s when we were trying to fill the position of the Director of our program. I remember one of the applicants indicated that he would be finishing his doctorate in about six months. Even if you discount a quarter of 600 applicants, you still have 450 qualified applicants. Choosing a career is a lot like this when you can literally do anything you want to do. You are lucky if you know what you want to do—"My great-grandfather was a doctor, my grandfather was a doctor, my dad is a doctor, and I am going to be a doctor." What about those first-generation college students who have no predestined path? They can do anything, but how do they choose? Sometimes the options are so overwhelming that they cannot decide even after they get into a doctoral program. I counseled with a young woman in our program and described the eight areas of concentration that were available to her in the program at that time. After I finished, she said okay. I asked okay, which one do you want to do? She said she wanted to do all of them. I explained that this was not feasible as it would require an extreme number of credit hours. She was almost distraught to hear this from me. She left the program long before she finished a single area of concentration—too many options.

8. Poor/Inadequate advisement—Throughout this book I have talked about and used examples of good and bad graduate advising. I could give literally dozens of examples of poor and inadequate advising that goes on in doctoral programs. Most of them have negative and some even dramatic consequences for the students involved. Essentially, in my experience there are at least four different types of poor and/or inadequate graduate advising. Most of these are caused by a lack of experience and mentoring in how to effectively advise doctoral students. There are a few, however, that are deliberate acts of sabotage, and while, no more damaging that most other forms, are highly unethical and should, when identified, be met with severe disciplinary action. Sadly, this is usually not the case. These forms and a brief discussion of each are presented in the following sections.

   a. Inexperience—Many of the errors I have witnessed in doctoral advising have been a function of a lack of experience in working with doctoral students. This includes me, especially early in my higher education career. In the chapter "Cutting Your Teeth," I identified the errors I made in working with my first doctoral advisee and truthfully these errors were a function of not knowing what to do or how to do it. I have encountered situations throughout my career in which I was faced with similar problems caused by ignorance, but now I know that I MUST help each student build a committee that compensates for my weaknesses. Sometimes this takes the form of a committee member with stronger expertise in a specific area of content or methodology, but sometimes it involves bringing a person onto the committee as a Co-Chair. It is not really fair to have a person added as a committee member but function more like a Co-Chair. I have taken this specific action as recently as within the past few years. A student who had asked me to serve as her committee chair was using a methodology that I just knew very little about. We had a junior faculty member in our program at the time that had studied this methodology with one of the leaders in the nation while he was pursuing his doctorate. I insisted that if she wanted me to chair the committee, we must persuade him to serve as a Co-Chair. He did agree to serve as a Co-Chair, and we were able to take care of her academic needs and he had the experience of Co-Chairing his first doctoral committee with an experienced doctoral advisor (yes, me). It seemed to be a Win-Win situation. Throughout most of my career I have been willing and even eager to help less experienced colleagues with their doctoral advising efforts. Sometimes my impetus for accepting this responsibility has been to help the student at their request, and at other times it has grown out of requests from colleagues to help them advise their doctoral students. For the most part, the outcome is the same. I have had a few instances of requests from students but met resistance from the faculty member. A few times, I have even met with the student at times which would enable us to avoid their major professor's knowledge that I was helping them. From my perspective, this situation usually grew out of insecurity or animosity toward me from the faculty member. Did I do the right thing to help them secretly? Maybe or maybe not—I THINK so, but you would have to judge this for yourself.

b. Priorities—Some faculty members just place student advising in a very low position on their prioritization of work responsibilities. This is especially problematic in Research Universities (RV/VH—Research University/Very High Research) because these are the institutions where the Publish or Perish world is at its most extreme form. Literally, if faculty do not publish, they will not be granted tenure and they will, consequently, be fired. I had a friend here at LSU who was a faculty member in another college and was a very good graduate advisor. He consistently placed students above research which resulted in him having few publications. He was denied tenure and went home that evening and committed suicide. Another young man who was a member of the faculty in our

School failed to publish adequately and was denied even a continuation of his appointment. At LSU, new faculty in tenure track positions receive an initial three-year appointment and then receive a second three-year appointment if they are making satisfactory progress toward tenure. He pursued positions at other universities but was unable to maintain employment in higher education. This bright, talented, skillful young man eventually took his own life. Based on these experiences, I always tell my young faculty members that they are NOT allowed to accept more than a few doctoral advisees, and I try very hard to avoid assigning them extra courses to teach (Sometimes this is unavoidable, but I always make sure they get extra compensation for the extra course.) until AFTER they are tenured. I see this as part of my responsibilities as their Department Head. Both of these young men left families including children that had to grow up without their dad. I never want to be associated with this happening again. I was not the Department Head for either of these men, but I cannot help but feel that there might have been things I could have done, especially with the one who was a colleague in my School. I do not accept my young faculty putting students in a position of low priority which is why I deliberately keep their advising load low. I will take on more advisees to avoid overloading my young faculty members.

There are faculty who take the position often described as "The university would be a great place to work if it were not for the students." I have worked with faculty members who took this attitude with their student advisees. I know of one young man who quit his job when he neared the dissertation phase of his program so that he could devote all his efforts to his study. He shared with me that he could not get one meeting per semester with his major professor. From a purely economic standpoint, this faculty member had six students enrolled in dissertation research credit (for an average of six semester credit hours each), which means that she should have been spending the equivalent of six hours per week on the course (three hours in class and three hours of preparation). This means that each of the six students enrolled should have been entitled to one hour per week of instructional time. I know that three of these six students did not have even one meeting per week for the semester regardless of the number of times they requested appointments. To be fair, this faculty member had a funded research grant during this time, but she received released time from her assigned courses for directing that grant. The bottom line is that the doctoral students were simply very low on her priority list. Oh yes, and this was a **tenured** faculty member. At the very end of the movie

"Teachers," Nick Nolte makes the point when talking about students that, "they're not here for us, we're here for them" (Levinson et al., 1984). The point is that if not for the students, faculty are not needed. Therefore, we should give them the priority and attention they need and deserve.

c. Overworked—Sometimes faculty members provide inadequate advisement for the doctoral students simply because they are overloaded with other work responsibilities. I do not mean to imply that it is okay, it is just a fact. I do not present this narrative by way of making excuses for what happens in these circumstances. It does, however, happen sometimes. This may take several forms. For example, I had a colleague in another department in our college who handled ALL the undergraduate advising for his department, and his department had almost 300 undergraduate students enrolled. His time was consumed by this responsibility, consequently he had few if any doctoral advisees, and when he did have a doctoral student, they got very little of his time. Other faculty are highly successful in acquiring externally funded research grants. It is true that their grant may provide a graduate assistantship for a doctoral student, but sometimes their efforts are directed totally toward getting the deliverables of the research grant accomplished. They may have little time to spend on the student's research, and sometimes they do not really want to spend time on the student's research—unless, of course, the grant research and the student's research are the same. On some occasions, the faculty overload takes the form of additional teaching responsibilities. There are times when I just cannot prevent my young faculty from having to teach extra courses. If this happens, do everything you can to, at least, get them some extra money for teaching an overload. Another colleague here at LSU was excessively active in college and university service activities. For example, he was a member of the University Athletic Council, he coordinated commencement activities for the University, he advised all undergraduate students in his department, he was a member of three college and university committees which included the College Faculty Policy Committee (Since he was the chair of the College committee, he represented the College on the University committee.) and the College Courses and Curriculum committee. I remember distinctly the meeting in which his Department Head was trying to convince the College Promotion Committee to approve him for promotion to the rank of Professor. His department head said that this faculty member had done everything he had been asked to do and all the things had been done very well. His department head went on the say that he had asked this faculty member to do "Damn near everything." He certainly had little or no time for doctoral advising. Oh yes, and he did NOT get promoted. A few years later he left LSU and accepted a position at Texas A & M University where they promoted him to Full Professor. They seemed to value his strengths more than we did at LSU. Probably the most common area for faculty to experience an overload that interferes with their graduate advising responsibilities is in research. This is especially true of young faculty but can happen with faculty at any rank. Sometimes this is unplanned such as a young faculty member applying for three different externally funded grants anticipating that one will be funded, but they get all three. Good news and bad news. The good news is that this is great for their curriculum vitae, the bad news is that now they have to complete the work of all three grants. In my third year here at LSU, I had applied for two different grants, and they were both funded. What I did not anticipate was that one of our faculty members accepted an upper-level administrative position here, and he specifically selected me to take over a major curriculum revision project focused on high school curricula in our field that had also been funded that year to him. Therefore, I had two grants for which I had applied, I had his grant, I had my normal teaching load, and I was assigned to assume his teaching load also. I had also agreed (before I knew about any of this) to serve as the faculty advisor for a very active student organization. I hardly saw my family at all that year. Another area of potential overload is an excessive number of doctoral students. For example, in 2009 I was serving as the Director of our School which is a 75% FTE appointment, I was teaching one course per semester which is (at least at LSU) considered a 25% FTE appointment, and I had 23 doctoral advisees 18 of whom were enrolled in dissertation research hours (9000 credit at LSU) which means that they were at least in the dissertation proposal writing stage of their program. Quite a few years ago, our director distributed to the faculty in our School a document that listed Gene M. Love from Pennsylvania State University as the author, something called the RICOP faculty workload guidelines. I have been unable to locate a copy of this document. I can only presume that it was an unpublished document that was shared with our Director by Dr. Love or someone else at Penn State. In any case, I do recall that this formula indicated that each doctoral advisee is the equivalent of an 8% FTE appointment. If you use only the students that were enrolled in dissertation research credit this is:

18 times .08 = 1.44
Administration = .75
Teaching = .25.

This equates to almost two and a half full-time jobs. Obviously, my students were not getting the attention they would have been receiving if I had been less overloaded. My point is just that you can get overloaded with doctoral advisees just like you can get overloaded with other aspects and assignments of your job. If I had it to do it over, would I have refused to work with some of these students?—Probably not. There are a few things I would have done differently, but mostly these things involve specific activities of directing my students' programs. Just in case you are interested: of the 18 students in dissertation research hours that semester, one left the program for personal reasons associated with his Father's untimely death (He tried to come back a few years later but was denied an extension.), four changed to another major professor with me remaining as a committee member (all four of these eventually graduated with their doctorate), and the other 13 graduated within a few semesters. Additionally, five doctoral students (not included in the 18) whom I was advising had graduated the previous academic year. Overall, 14 of my doctoral advisees graduated in a two-year period.

Getting rid of a student—Sadly, I must admit that I have personally witnessed graduate advisors taking actions that were very deliberate attempts to rid the program of a student that they did not believe should be allowed to continue. I have discussed earlier in the book students who were expelled from other programs for various reasons that ended up in our program and performed very well. One was pressured into pleading guilty of plagiarism on his general examination (which was not true—I saw the original exam) on the promise that he would be re-admitted after he sat out one semester. When he tried to return, he was denied admission because he had confessed to plagiarism. This was done (according to a faculty member in that department) as a technique to reduce doctoral enrollments since that department had lost some positions to budget cuts.

Another student in another department was failed on his general exam because his major professor (with whom he worked closely) was a jerk and left the university. Afterward no one wanted to work with the student, and to resolve that problem of his enrollment in the program, they simply voted to fail him on his general exam. The Graduate School Dean's Representative did not agree with the decision of the committee. The student came to our program and performed so well on his general exam that his Dean's Representative (not the same one from his previous program) sent a memo to the Dean of the Graduate School commending him on his performance and our program on the quality of our process.

These examples are from other programs, and it seems all too easy for me to point fingers at them. However, remember the scripture in the Bible which says,

> "³And why beholdest thou the mote that is in thy brother's eye, but considerest not the beam that is in thine own eye?
>
> ⁴ Or how wilt thou say to thy brother, Let me pull out the mote out of thine eye; and, behold, a beam [is] in thine own eye?
>
> ⁵ Thou hypocrite, first cast out the beam out of thine own eye; and then shalt thou see clearly to cast out the mote out of thy brother's eye." (Bible)

I cite this to acknowledge that our program is not blameless when it comes to this type of action. I have already mentioned several incidents in our program that centered around attempts to "get rid" of students. This has ranged from as little as a faculty member simply saying that this student does not belong here and should be dropped from the program using whatever means are required to a faculty member specifically planning the best technique to remove a student from the program. When I was the head of the program, I tried to hold a line against unfair treatment of students, but obviously I was not completely successful. One of the worst examples was a student who had a very mediocre general exam and could easily have received a negative vote. I personally witnessed the discussion in which the committee members considered that they did not want him to get a doctorate from the program. If they voted to fail him on the exam, they would have had to give him a second chance to pass the exam. Therefore, they made the decision that the best way to ensure that he did not get the degree was to vote to pass him on the general exam and then just make sure that he never received approval on a dissertation topic. Oh, by the way, they were successful in this endeavor. Disgusting, isn't it?

> Another example involved multiple faculty members engaging in what could only be described as an assault in the student's proposal meeting. This young woman answered every question very well and was still denied approval of her proposal. I have a strong suspicion that two of the committee members had planned before the meeting to be sure that the student was unsuccessful. I can understand the lack of experience causing errors to be made in graduate advising. I have been there myself, and some of the errors were significantly detrimental to students. However, deliberately setting out to make a student fail an exam or be unsuccessful in the program is, in my opinion, reprehensible. Once you make the commitment to admit the student you are obligated to do whatever you can (within the rules of the institution and ethical principles) to help the student be successful in completing the program. You will have some students who just cannot make it through the program. However, you should be able to examine yourself and be comfortable that you did all you could to help them be successful. If not, I challenge you to avoid having to reach this conclusion again with another student.

LESSON NUMBER 15: GIVE YOUR "TOP" STUDENTS THE SAME ATTENTION AND ASSISTANCE THAT YOU GIVE TO OTHER STUDENTS. THEY NEED IT AND DESERVE IT

It is inevitable that you occasionally have a student who leaves the program without finishing the degree. There are cases when this is simply the best thing to do. However, I personally find it especially sad when the person is fully capable of finishing the degree and just does not complete

CHAPTER 16

SEE YOU WHEN YOU GET BACK—PERSONAL PRIORITIES

There are times when you simply must do what you want to do or risk never being able to do this thing at all in life. I am an avid New York Yankees fan. I am a baseball fan sort of, but I am a big Yankees fan. One thing that I always wanted to do was see a game in Yankee stadium. I waited and waited and waited for a time when it was convenient for me to go, and now Yankee stadium has been torn down. Oh, I know I could still go to the "New" Yankee stadium, but it would not be the same. I wanted to actually sit in the stands of the "House that Ruth built." I wanted to be where Lou Gehrig, Joe Dimaggio, and Mickey Mantle played. Almost every great player who played the game stepped into that batter's box. I have a two-foot by three-foot print of Babe Ruth hitting the "Called shot" displayed in my office. If you do not know the story of the called shot, look it up. It is fun to read about.

Well, to the point, I was working with a man who was very near 50 years old and was an avid cyclist. He commuted to campus about 10 miles each day, and he did it most days on his bicycle. He was offered the opportunity to lead a cross-country bicycle trek made up of people from all over the world, but it would cause him to miss final exam week in May and be gone for just over three months. He clearly wanted to go, but some of his professors strongly discouraged it saying that he needed to decide if he wanted a doctorate or not. As his advisor and one of his instructors that Spring semester, I encouraged him to go if it was something he really wanted to do. Essentially, it was likely to be his last chance to lead such a group because of his age. He took his other exams early since his professors refused to assign him an "Incomplete" grade so that he could finish his requirements when he returned for the next Fall semester. He made "C" grades in two courses, but since he earned an "A" in both of his other courses (one of which was mine—he was a very good student), his GPA for the semester was above 3.0 and thus he was not even placed on probation. This tour he led started at the Atlantic Ocean on the coast of Virginia and just over three months later the group arrived at the Pacific Ocean on the coast of Oregon. They had no trailing vehicle and had only the supplies they could carry in their backpacks and in the one small trailer pulled by the leader (which was him). If he had waited the three years until he completed the degree, he may never have been able to complete this quest. As it is, he completed both this task that he had long wanted to do and his doctorate. Oh, he may have finished the degree a semester later than he might have, and certainly his GPA was a little lower, but you be the judge. Did he make the right decision? I thought so at the time, and I still do. Not only this, but I did anything I could to support him in this endeavor. I was not able to do much, but I did tell him to focus on his other courses and not worry about mine. I told him he could finish it when he got back, and he did. He earned an "A" in his statistics course, an "A" in my course, and "C" grades in both of his other major courses.

Another student with whom I worked, was nearing the end of her program when she received an invitation that she found just too good to pass up. She was of Scandinavian descent, and she had a very large extended family, some of whom were still in Norway and Denmark. They had planned a huge family reunion on a cruise ship that was going north and, for a time, would be north of the Artic circle. It was, of course, a summer event. This was the first time they had undertaken such an event in her lifetime, and she did not know if she would ever have another chance to participate in something like this. It inevitably delayed her graduation by a semester, but she was very clear that it was well worth the delay. She said that (as expected) the sun never set while they were that far north. As she described to me, she went out on deck at 3:00 a.m. and the sun was still visible on the horizon.

The point here is that sometimes life forcibly interferes in students' planned timelines, and then sometimes students choose to allow events to interfere. It is very important that you make certain that you explain to the student, so that they will be aware of the impact their interruption will have on their academic progress, but do not try to control their decision. The circumstances with which these two students were faced seemed very easy decisions to me. In fact, I HOPE that if I had been presented with either of these choices, I would have made the same decision they did.

LESSON NUMBER 16: SOMETIMES PERSONAL OPPORTUNITIES BECOME PRIORITIES AND MAY SLOW YOUR STUDENT'S PROGRESS

If your student asks for your input on these matters, be open and honest with them. However, remember that it is not your decision. The student going to her family reunion did not ask my opinion, but she did discuss it with me. The student going on the cross-country bicycle trip did ask my opinion, and we discussed it in depth. I would have advised both of them to GO, and in fact, I did advise the cyclist to take the trip. Neither of these students was facing an imminent expiration of their time limit; therefore, the decisions were easier than if they had been. My advice might have been different if the student WAS facing the end of their allowable time to complete the degree. Another student was preparing to defend her dissertation and was invited to accompany the University Administration on the University airplane to see the Tigers play in the College Baseball World Series. This was during the 1990s when Skip Bertman was the Head Coach and LSU owned the Baseball National Championship. They won five championships in a ten-year period. She was a huge college baseball fan, and rarely missed an LSU home game. I explained that taking more than a week away at this specific moment would mean that she would graduate a semester later, but she said it was worth it to her. I offered to take her place if she wanted to stay and work on her dissertation (just kidding). Besides, I would not have been next on their list if she had declined. She did go, and LSU did win the national championship and who knows maybe it was because she was there cheering for them—Okay I realize that is silly. The point is that it was her decision, and my job was to be sure that she knew the consequences. Oh yes, and she did graduate—it was a semester later, but she did graduate.

CHAPTER 17

REFERENCES

King James Version. Bible. Matthew 7:3-5.
King James Version. Bible. Matthew 7:12.
Carter, J. (1989). *Nasty people: How to stop being hurt by them without becoming one of them*. Contemporary Books.
Gewirtz, P. (1995–1996). On 'I know it when i see it.' HeinOnLine 105 Yale I. J.
Idioms, The. (n.d.). *If wishes were horses, beggars would ride*. https://www.theidioms.com/if-wishes-were-horses-beggars-would-ride/
Ky Phrase: Learn about Phrases and Sayings, "You Can't Judge a Book by Its Cover." https://knowyourphrase.com/you-cant-judge-a-book-by-its-cover. (Retrieved January 25, 2021)
Levinson, A., Russo, A., Russo, I. (Producers) & Hiller, A. (Director). (1984). *Teachers* [Motion Picture]. United States: United Artists.
Sutton, R. I. (2007). *The No Asshole Rule*. Warner Business Books.
Zavaleta, J. (2010, February 26). *Heisman curse: Myth or fact*. https://bleacherreport.com/articles/353179-heisman-curse-myth-or-fact